P9-AEV-322

WITHDRAWN

Workshop Creations

Classic Woodworking Projects for Indoors & Outdoors

SHADY OAK PRESS

Workshop Creations
Classic Woodworking Projects for Indoors & Outdoors

Copyright © 2007 Shady Oak Press

All rights reserved. No part of this publication may be reproduced, stored in an electronic retrieval system or transmitted in any form or by any (electronic, mechanical, photocopying, recording or otherwise) without the prior written permission of the copyright owner.

Tom Carpenter
Creative Director

Jen Weaverling
Production Editor

Steve Foley
Book Design and Production

Contributing Builders: Dan Cary, John Nadeau, Luke Rennie

Contributing Illustrator: Gabriel Graphics

Contributing Photographers: Mike Anderson, Neal Barrett, Dan Cary, Fuller Focus, Alan Geho, Scott Jacobson. Mark Johanson, Bill King, Mark Macemon, Phil Leisenheimer and Larry Okrend

Contributing Project Designer: Wayne Sutter

Contributing Writers: Neal Barrett, Mike Berger, Dan Cary, Vern Grassel, Raoul Hennin, Joe Hurst-Wajszczuk, Mark Johanson, Chris Marshall and Larry Okrend

Production Assistance: Brad Classson

Special thanks to: Mike Billstein, Terry Casey and Janice Cauley.

1 2 3 4 5 6 7 8 9 10 / 12 11 10 09 08 07
© 2007 North American Membership Group
ISBN: 918-1-58159-342-6

Distributed by:
Sterling Publishing Co., Inc.
387 Park Avenue South
New York, NY 10016-8810

For information about custom editions, special sales, premium and corporate purchases, please contact Sterling Special Sales Department at 800-805-5489 or specialsales@sterlingpub.com.

For your safety, caution and good judgment should be used when following instructions described in this book. Take into consideration your level of skill and the safety precautions related to the tools and materials shown. Neither the publisher, Shady Oak Press, nor any of its affiliates can assume responsibility for any damage to property or persons as a result of the misuse of the information provided. Consult your local building department for information on permits, codes, regulations and laws that may apply to your project.

SHADY OAK PRESS

12301 Whitewater Drive
Minnetonka, MN 55343

Contents

Introduction

There's nothing like spending a morning, afternoon or evening in the workshop. No matter what life has been throwing at you lately, a few hours with wood, power tools, hand tools, sandpaper, screws, nails and stain can give you a whole new attitude ... and some wonderful creations to show off both indoors and out.

As woodworkers, we can always use more good project ideas to pull us into the shop for a few hours "away." So here in these pages are over two dozen all-time-great projects from the woodworking experts and editors at Shady Oak Press.

Start indoors, with projects ranging from a tasteful gateleg table and a wall desk everybody wants for their own, to plantation shutters, a curved cook's rack (we make the bending process easy) and a very traditional storage rack that you can put to a very modern use. Then move to the great outdoors with an easy glider, a functional yet beautiful deck bench, a summer seat specially made for two, and a sports caddy to keep the kids' or grandkids' stuff neat and together. We've even included some projects that will help make your shop a better organized and more efficient place to work.

Of course, we also made sure that you won't suffer through any guesswork when it comes time to get going on your creations. Detailed diagrams, complete materials lists, helpful shopping lists and clear step-by-step instructions (brought to you in both concise words and instructive full-color photographs) assure that you work through every project smoothly and successfully.

And in the end, that's what it's all about — a project that looks great and serves its purpose, and was also a joy to make. Yes, when a project is a very special *Workshop Creation* made with your own hands, it truly is something special.

SHADY OAK PRESS

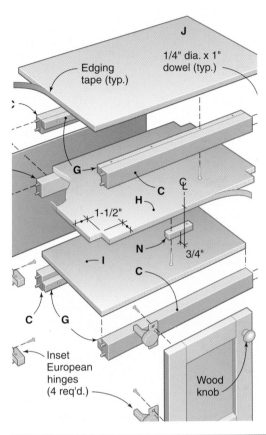

Edging tape (typ.)

J

1/4" dia. x 1" dowel (typ.)

G

C

H

C L

1-1/2"

N

3/4"

I

C

C

G

Inset European hinges (4 req'd.)

Wood knob

Chapter 1
Indoors

Gateleg Table

Traditionally, gateleg tables share two general design elements: They are small (tea-table or occasional-table size) and have round or oval tops. When we decided to resurrect the gateleg approach, we deliberately disregarded tradition, choosing instead to make a large, rectangular-top kitchen table with a drop leaf at each end. The resulting table has a top that's generously proportioned to make it useful even when the leaves are down, but it's compact enough to fit into a small alcove or up against a wall. With the leaves extended, the table can seat six diners comfortably. Because each end has not one but two gatelegs, you can slide chairs under the table on all sides. The gateleg pairs also provide more stability and support than a single gateleg or a pull-out drop-leaf support.

Gateleg Table

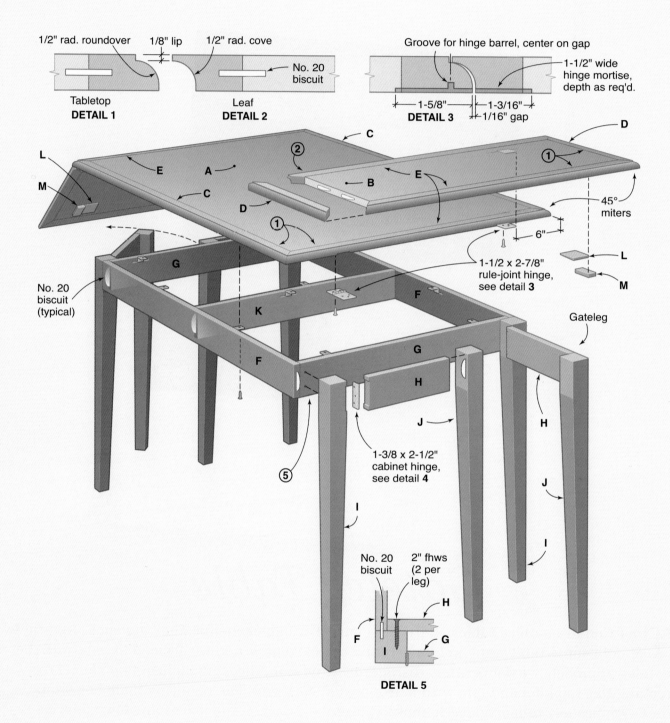

1/2" rad. roundover   1/8" lip   1/2" rad. cove

No. 20 biscuit

Tabletop
DETAIL 1

Leaf
DETAIL 2

Groove for hinge barrel, center on gap

1-1/2" wide hinge mortise, depth as req'd.

1-5/8"   1-3/16"
DETAIL 3   1/16" gap

C

②

L

M

E   A

B

E

D

C

D

①

①

D

45° miters

1-1/2 x 2-7/8" rule-joint hinge, see detail **3**

6"

L

M

No. 20 biscuit (typical)

G

K

F

F

G

H

Gateleg

H

J

H

①

⑤

1-3/8 x 2-1/2" cabinet hinge, see detail **4**

J

I

I

No. 20 biscuit

2" fhws (2 per leg)

H

F

G

I

DETAIL 5

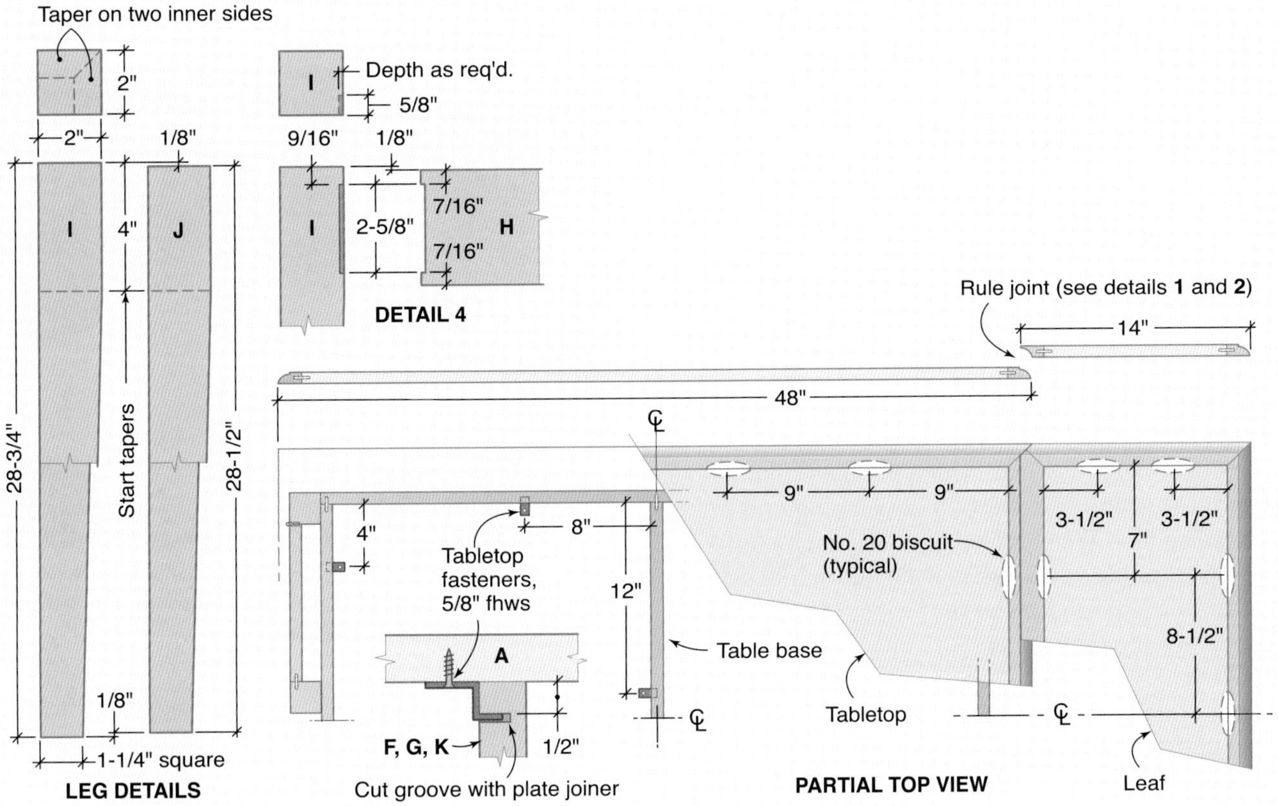
Taper on two inner sides
2"
2"
1/8"
I
4"
J
Start tapers
28-3/4"
28-1/2"
1/8"
1-1/4" square
LEG DETAILS
I
Depth as req'd.
5/8"
9/16"
1/8"
I
2-5/8"
7/16"
7/16"
H
DETAIL 4
Rule joint (see details 1 and 2)
14"
48"
℄
4"
8"
Tabletop fasteners, 5/8" fhws
12"
A
F, G, K
1/2"
Cut groove with plate joiner
Table base
9"
9"
No. 20 biscuit (typical)
Tabletop
3-1/2"
3-1/2"
7"
8-1/2"
℄
Leaf
PARTIAL TOP VIEW

Shopping List

- ☐ ¾-in. × 4×8 sheet MDF-core plain-sliced maple veneer plywood (1)
- ☐ 10 bf 10/4 hard maple (for eight legs)
- ☐ 14 bf 4/4 hard maple, for 25 ft. of ⅞ × 1½-in. trim and 20 ft. of ¾ × 3½-in. rail
- ☐ 2½ × 1⅜-in. cabinet hinges (4)
- ☐ 1½ × 2⅞-in. rule-joint hinges (2)
- ☐ Table clips (10)

Materials

	Part/Description	No.	Size
A	Tabletop, veneered MDF	1	¾ × 31 × 45 in.
B	Leaves, veneered MDF	2	¾ × 11 × 31 in.
C	Banding	2	¾ × 1½ × 48 in.**
D	Banding	4	¾ × 1½ × 14 in.**
E	Banding	6	¾ × 1½ × 34 in.**
F	Front/back rails	2	¾ × 3½ × 42½ in.
G	End rails	2	¾ × 3½ × 27 in.
H	Swing rails	4	¾ × 3⅜ × 10 in.
I	Legs	4	2 × 2 × 28¾ in.
J	Gatelegs	4	2 × 2 × 28½ in.
K	Spreader	1	¾ × 3½ × 27 in.
L	Leveling wedges	4	¼ × 2 × 2 in.
M	Stop blocks	4	⅜ × 1 × 2 in.

*All parts solid maple except as noted
**Finished size, see text

Lay out the tabletop and leaves on sheet stock. Cut them to rough size with a circular saw and then to final size on the table saw. The grain runs in the same direction on all parts.

We used hard maple for the table base and maple-veneered medium density fiberboard (MDF) for the tabletop and leaves. MDF-core sheet stock is denser than veneer-core plywood, which makes it more stable and less prone to deflection or warping and gives it a heavier feel. We chose sheet stock with plain-sawn hard maple veneer that looks more like solid wood than the more typical (but considerably cheaper) rotary-cut veneer.

MAKE THE TOP AND LEAVES

To begin, cut the tabletop and leaves to rough size from heavy MDF-core sheet stock (**Photo A**). Then cut them to final size on your table saw. (We used a 40-tooth blade on our circular saw and an 80-tooth blade on our table saw.) Try to cut the pieces so all four sides have freshly cut edges.

The leaves and tabletop are banded with 1½-in.-wide maple strips to conceal the edges. You have a couple of milling options when making the banding. The easier way is to plane and joint your banding stock so it's exactly the same thickness as the MDF stock. By using biscuits to align the banding strips, you should be able to get a pretty clean fit. But if you're a little more particular and you want to guarantee that your banding strips are exactly flush with the top and bottom surfaces of the MDF, mill the strips so they're slightly thicker than the MDF — about ⅞ in. Then after you attach them, trim them — either by sanding or by using a router and flush-trimming bit. We chose the latter approach. It turned out to be a bit cumbersome, but our effort resulted in nice, flush seams.

To trim the banding, first attach a tall auxiliary fence to your router table fence. The bottom of the auxiliary fence should be far enough above the surface of the router table to provide clearance for the banding (at least 1¾ in.). Mount a piloted flush-cutting bit in your router table — we used a 2-in. bit to

After mitering the corners of the 1½-in.-wide banding strips, attach two opposing strips with No. 20 biscuits; then trim the banding flush with the surfaces of the tabletop and leaves using a 2-in.-long flush-cutting bit.

trim our 1½-in. banding strips. Adjust the fence so it's aligned exactly with the outside edge of the bearing on the piloted bit. Then feed the panel through the bit after the banding strip is attached, pressing the surface of the panel against the fence.

When framing a panel, trim each banding strip before the adjoining untrimmed strip is attached. Otherwise, the untrimmed strip will catch on the auxiliary fence, throwing off the cut. We cut all of our miters before flush-trimming, taping each banding strip in place once all the miters fit. Then we labeled

Attach the second set of opposing strips as shown here, again using No. 20 biscuits and glue. Once the glue is dry, run this banding through the router table as before. Repeat the process until you have finished all three panels.

With a piloted ½-in. roundover bit, cut the profile in all four edges of the tabletop and in all but the hinge edges of the leaves. Don't try to cut the entire profile in a single pass — you'll need to make at least two or three passes.

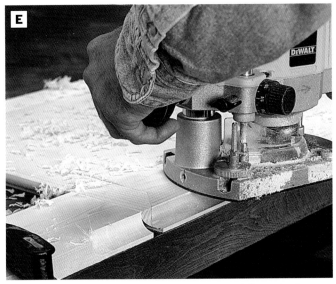

Cut cove profiles in the hinge edges of the leaves. Make test cuts on scrap wood first until the router is set up so the coved board fits snugly together with the roundovers on the hinge edges of the tabletop (see next photo).

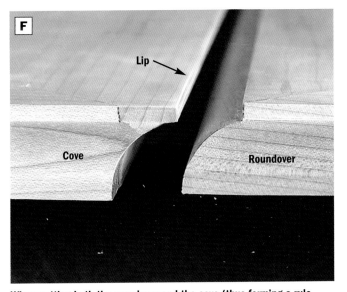

When cutting both the roundover and the cove (thus forming a rule joint), make sure the mating parts fit together snugly, with the tops and bottoms flush. Leave a lip (⅛ to ¼ in.) at the top of each edge.

and removed the strips. We attached two opposing strips to each panel using glue and No. 20 biscuits. Once the glue set, we ran the strips through the flush-cutting bit on both faces (**Photo B**). Then we attached the second set of opposing strips and ran them through, repeating until all three panels were framed (**Photo C**).

Once you've attached all the banding, cut the edge profiles and the rule joints. Start by mounting a piloted ½-in. roundover bit in your router. Cut a roundover in all four edges of the large tabletop, leav-

ing a ⅛-in. lip at the top of each cut. Also round over the end and short edges of each leaf, leaving the longer edge that will mate against the tabletop uncut. You'll need to make a minimum of two passes on each cut, deepening the cut after each pass (**Photo D**).

Make a ½-in. cove cut on the mating edge of each leaf (**Photo E**). This cut should also leave a ⅛- to ¼-in.-thick lip at the top edge. Make the cove cuts a little at a time, checking the fit of the coved edge against the mating roundover cut on the tabletop edge (**Photo F**). Cut until the matching parts fit

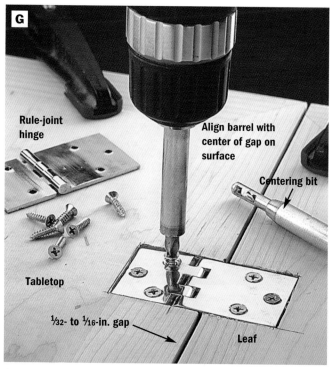

Cut mortises for the rule-joint hinges, remembering to allow for the hinge barrels. Use spacers between the tabletop and leaves to create a consistent ¹⁄₃₂- to ¹⁄₁₆-in. gap.

Cut tapers in two adjoining faces of each leg, starting 24¾ in. from the leg bottom. The bottoms of the legs should measure 1¼ × 1¼ in. after the tapers are cut. We used a tapering jig and table saw to make the taper cuts.

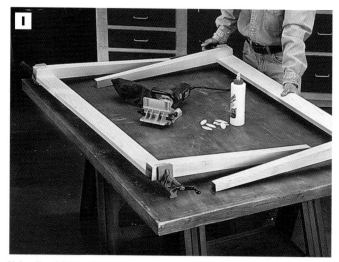

Using No. 20 biscuits and glue, attach a pair of legs to each end of each front/back rail. The outer face of each rail should be flush with the outer faces of the legs. Make sure the tapered faces of the legs meet at the inside corner.

together perfectly, forming the rule joint.

Next, attach the rule-joint hinges to the tabletop and leaves. Use a pair of hinges at each joint, positioning the hinges so the near edge is 6 in. from the tabletop and leaf edges.

To lay out hinge locations, set the tabletop and leaves upside down on a flat surface. Press the rule joints together; then separate them by ¹⁄₃₂ to ¹⁄₁₆ in. to provide joint clearance. Position the hinges so they're parallel with the joint and the hinge barrels are centered on the seam of the rule joint on the top side of the tabletop. Outline the hinge plates on the tabletop and leaves. Cut the mortises with a sharp chisel — note that the mortises for the short plates should start about ¾ in. from the mating edges of the tabletop. You'll need to cut a shallow groove in the tabletop mortise to house the hinge barrel. Attach the hinges with ¾-in. screws driven into pilot holes **(Photo G).** Use a centering bit to drill the pilot holes.

MAKE THE LEGS

To begin making the legs, plane ¹⁰⁄₄ maple to 2 in. thick; then rip it into 2-in.-wide strips. (You could laminate thinner strips of maple into blanks if you prefer.) Cut all eight legs to a rough length of at least 30 in.

Lay out tapers in the two adjacent edges of each leg. The tapered legs will be 1¼ × 1¼ in. at the bottoms and gradually increase to the full 2 × 2-in. thickness 24¾ in. from the bottom. To cut the tapers **(Photo H),** we used a table saw and taper-cutting jig. You could also use your jointer or a band saw.

Once you've cut the tapers, cut all eight legs to 28¾ in. long, resulting in 4 in. of untapered stock at the top of each leg. Then trim ⅛ in. off each end of

Cut biscuit slots for joining the rail/leg assemblies to the end rails. (Remove the fence from the biscuit joiner to cut the slots for the legs.) Cut biscuit slots for the spreader that fits between the front and back rails as well.

Glue up the table base assembly. Check to make sure the legs are square to the rails, and adjust as necessary. Clamp until dry.

four of the legs (the gatelegs). Making the gatelegs slightly shorter prevents them from touching the floor when the table leaves are down — otherwise, the table will rock.

MAKE THE TABLE BASE

Now that the legs are completed, you can begin the table base. Plane and rip stock to thickness and width; then cut the front/back rails, end rails, swing rails and spreader to length. Attach a fixed leg to each end of the front and back rails. The legs should be flush with the rail ends and tops. Make sure the legs and rails are perpendicular and the tapered faces meet in the inside corner. Join the legs to the rails with glue and No. 20 biscuits (**Photo I**).

Position the end rails and spreader between the leg/rail assemblies. Cut slots for biscuit joints (**Photo J**); then glue and clamp the joints, checking to make sure the assembly is square (**Photo K**). For extra reinforcement, drive a pair of No. 8 × 2-in. flathead wood screws through the inside faces of the end rails into each leg.

Next, make the swing rails. Attach the gatelegs to the swing rails using glue and biscuits (**Photo L**). The tops of the swing rails should be flush with the tops of the gatelegs, and the faces should be flush.

Cut mortises for your cabinet hinges in the free

With No. 20 biscuits and glue, attach the swing rails flush with the tops of the gatelegs. Make sure to trim ⅛ in. from the end of each gateleg first, and note that the swing rails are ⅛ in. narrower than the fixed rails.

ends of the swing rails and in the inside faces of the fixed legs. Position the hinges so the bottom edges of the swing rails are flush with the bottom edges of the end rails, creating a ⅛-in. gap between the tops of the swing rails and the tops of the fixed rails. (This will provide clearance for the swing rails and allow you to level the leaves.) Screw the hinges to the swing rail ends and then to the fixed legs (**Photo M**).

Cut mortises for the swing rail butt hinges, making sure to center the hinge plate top-to-bottom on the swing rail. Use a centering bit to drill pilot holes for the hinge screws; then attach the hinges.

Use table clips to attach the tabletop to the table base. Drive ⅝-in. screws through the clips and into the tabletop. Make sure the top is centered on the base and that the leaves have clearance to swing.

ADJUST AND LEVEL

Set the assembly upright; then swing the gatelegs open. Use a framing square or straightedge to adjust the gatelegs until the swing rails are parallel with the front and back rails. Outline the position of the gatelegs on the undersides of the table leaves.

Bevel-rip a 2-in.-wide strip of maple so it's ¼ in. thick on one edge and ⅛ in. thick on the other. Cross-cut the strip so you have four 2 × 2-in. pieces to serve as leveling wedges for the leaves. Slip each wedge between the bottom of the leaf and the top of a gate-leg, leading with the thin edge of the wedge. (Make sure the legs match up with the outlines you made on the tabletop.) Adjust the wedge position so the leaf is level with the tabletop. Trace a cutting line onto each wedge by following the edge of the gateleg (**Photo O).** Trim each wedge along the cutting line; then glue the wedges to the undersides of the leaves. Test the fit when the glue is dry: You may need to attach leveling feet to the gateleg bottoms, depending on how flat your floor is.

To prevent the gatelegs from swinging open too far, cut thin stop blocks and glue them next to the wedges, away from the direction of swing.

Finally, sand thoroughly and apply your finish of choice. We sprayed satin-finish waterborne lacquer with an HVLP sprayer.

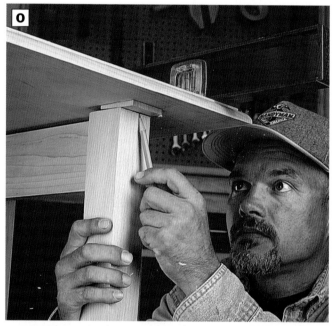

Open the table and adjust the level of each leaf by slipping a wedge between the top of each leg and the underside of the leaf. Adjust the wedge until the leaf is level. Mark the position of the wedge, trim it to size and glue it in place.

ATTACH THE TABLETOP

We used table clips to attach the MDF-core tabletop to the table base. We cut the grooves for the clips with a biscuit joiner. Once the grooves are cut, lay the tabletop and leaves upside down in an open position on a flat surface. Position the table base on the underside of the tabletop, adjusting so the overhang is equal at the front and back and on the ends. Attach the tabletop by driving ⅝-in. flathead wood screws through the guide holes in the table clips and into the underside of the tabletop (**Photo N).** Do not use glue.

Mark Johanson, *writer*
Dan Cary, *photo production*
Mark Macemon, *photographer*
John Nadeau, *builder*

Lookin' Good

Unlike a picture frame, which should complement the
work it holds, a mirror frame must be attractive enough
to stand on its own. At the same time, a mirror frame works
best when it harmonizes or blends with its surroundings.
This frame was designed to have a classic architectural look,
rather than a decorative style.

Lookin' Good

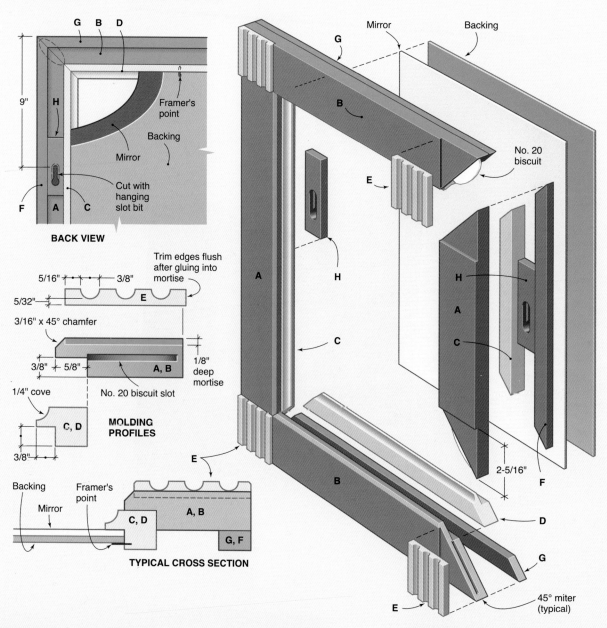

BACK VIEW

9"

G B D

Framer's point

Backing

Mirror

Cut with hanging slot bit

F A C

MOLDING PROFILES

Trim edges flush after gluing into mortise

5/16" 3/8"

5/32"

E

3/16" x 45° chamfer

3/8" 5/8"

A, B

1/8" deep mortise

No. 20 biscuit slot

1/4" cove

C, D

3/8"

TYPICAL CROSS SECTION

Backing

Framer's point

Mirror

C, D

A, B

G, F

Mirror

Backing

G

B

E

A

H

C

B

E

G

No. 20 biscuit

H

A

C

F

2-5/16"

D

G

45° miter (typical)

E

Materials and Cutting List			
Part/Description	**No.**	**Size**	
A Molding sides, cherry	2	$3/4 \times 2^{1/2} \times 28$ in.	
B Molding top/bottom, cherry	2	$3/4 \times 2^{1/2} \times 22$ in.	
C Side coves, maple	2	$3/4 \times 1 \times 24^{1/2}$ in.*	
D Top/bottom coves, maple	2	$3/4 \times 1 \times 18^{3/16}$ in.*	
E Corner plaques, maple	4	$5/16 \times 2^{5/16} \times 2^{5/16}$ in.*	
F Side strips, cherry	2	$3/8 \times 3/4 \times 28$ in.	
G Top/bottom strips, cherry	2	$3/8 \times 3/4 \times 22$ in.	
H Hanger blocks, cherry	2	$3/8 \times 1^{1/8} \times 4$ in.	
I Mirror and backing	1	$1/8 \times 16^{7/8} \times 22^{7/8}$ in.	

*Cut to fit after assembling outside frame.

Shopping List

- ☐ 3 bf cherry
- ☐ 1 bf maple
- ☐ Mirror (see cutting list)
- ☐ Backer (1/8-in. hardboard)
- ☐ No. 20 biscuits
- ☐ Yellow glue
- ☐ Framer's points

One of the most versatile approaches to frame making is to use nesting moldings. By combining a variety of molding patterns, you can create different styles. The more moldings you nest together, the deeper the frame appears. Conversely, if you stack moldings from the outside to the inside, the center of the frame projects rather than recedes.

You can also combine different woods and molding sizes to create a frame with more depth and visual appeal. I used cherry for this frame's larger outside molding and maple for the inside cove molding and corner plaques. The contrast and color differences between cherry and maple are slight at first but

intensify as the cherry darkens with age. Other attractive wood combinations are oak with ash and mahogany with walnut.

Before you start on this project, keep in mind that you can modify the size of your frame to suit its function. For instance, I made this entryway mirror just large enough to reflect a visitor's head and shoulders.

MAKE MOLDING

Using the proper sequence when milling frame stock can be the difference between success and failure. Cutting out of order can prevent you from safely completing the molding or leave a ragged edge. Setting up your tools properly also contributes to precision — but more important, it ensures safety. For the best results, follow the steps shown in the photos and outlined below.

I often buy rough, oversize stock and mill it to the required thickness for a project. However, because not every Club member owns a jointer and a planer, I designed this project to be made out of ¾-in.-thick

First cut the rabbet in the molding stock. Be sure to use featherboards and a hold-down to prevent kickback.

Next, chamfer the molding edge on a router table. Use featherboards to ensure a smooth cut.

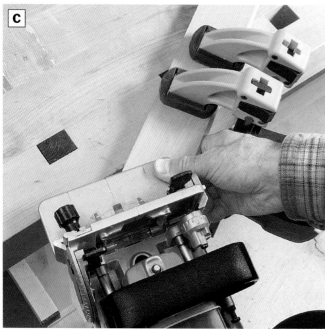

Miter the ends of the molding and then cut centered biscuit slots. Be sure the stock is clamped securely to the bench.

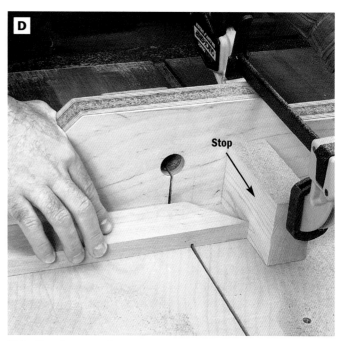

Make the plaque-mortise shoulder cuts with a sliding table on your table saw. Use a stop block for consistent cuts.

To remove the mortise waste, cut slowly with the band saw or make repeated passes on the table saw.

Cut the channels in the plaque stock with a 3/16-in.-radius core box bit. Rout the center channel last.

stock that's available at any home center. To get the 1⅛-in. finished thickness for the molding, I glued ⅜-in.-thick strips to the back of the frame. These strips were simply the waste from trimming the molding to width. To have enough waste, you'll need to buy boards that are at least an inch wider than the finished molding.

Frames don't require much stock, so matching wood is a luxury you can easily afford. Cut all the

frame's stock out of a single board so the color and grain will match perfectly. If you rip a board in half, orient the ripped edges to face each other when you assemble the frame so the grain appears balanced.

Once you've ripped the molding to the proper width, cut the rabbets (**Photo A**) in both the cherry and maple (cove) moldings. Use featherboards and hold-downs as needed, particularly with smaller stock that can chatter or rise off the blade. I prefer to

Resaw the plaque stock in half; then plane or sand the back flat to bring it to the correct thickness.

cut rabbets on the table saw rather than on a router table because router bits can splinter the edge of the stock. The table saw fitted with a good combination blade (such as a 50-tooth ATB with raker) always produces a clean edge.

Use a router table to cut the chamfer, cove and channels in the moldings (see drawing and photos). I used three common router bits for these cuts: a 45-degree chamfer bit, a ¼-in. cove bit (both with ball-bearing pilots) and a ³⁄₁₆-in.-radius core-box bit. You probably have these bits in your collection, but if you don't, you can substitute bits with similar profiles.

DETAILS AND JOINERY

To make the corner plaques, start with a ¾ × 2⁵⁄₁₆-in. piece that's about 12 in. long. The thicker stock makes it safer to rout the channels (Photo F). Once you've routed the channels, resaw and then sand or plane the stock to the final ⁵⁄₁₆-in. thickness. Then you can cut the plaques to size.

Before you cut miters on your finished cherry stock, make test cuts on a scrap piece of the same thickness and width. Unless your saw is making true 45-degree cuts, either the inside or outside corner of the miters will be open when the frame is assembled. To test, make a 45-degree cut in the center of the

scrap piece; then turn one half over and make a second cut. (This creates a V-shaped waste piece.) Abut the mitered ends of the two halves to form a straight edge. If the edge isn't straight, you'll need to adjust your saw. Don't cut the miters on the maple cove stock until you've assembled the cherry molding.

I used No. 20 biscuits to join the miters. Biscuits make strong joints and align parts precisely. If you don't have a plate joiner, you'll need to fasten the miters with dowels, wood splines or even plugged screws. Glue alone won't hold on the miter's end grain.

You can cut the mortises for the corner plaques as I did, by first making a shoulder cut on the table saw and then removing the waste on the band saw. Or you can remove the waste by making repeated passes on the table saw. The mortise bottom must be flat and smooth to glue on the corner plaques.

ASSEMBLE AND FINISH

Sand all the cherry parts with 120-grit paper before assembly. Be sure the parts fit together properly before gluing, and check that the assembly is square by measuring diagonally from corner to corner.

Once the glue has dried, cut the maple (nesting) moldings to fit; then glue them in place. If you plan

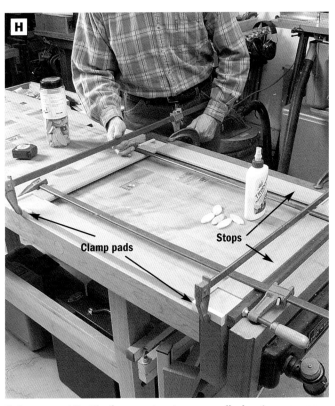

Before assembling the frame, set up two perpendicular stops on your bench to keep the stock square when clamping.

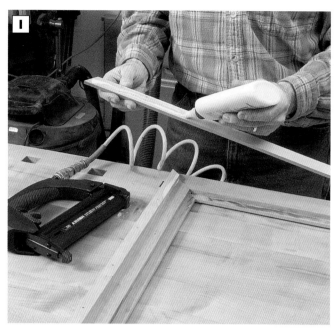

Glue and brad-nail the strips F, G to the back of the frame. The strips give the frame a thicker profile.

Cut each nesting cove molding individually to ensure a tight fit; then glue the moldings into the rabbet.

Bevel the edges of the corner plaques and glue them in position with the channels running vertically.

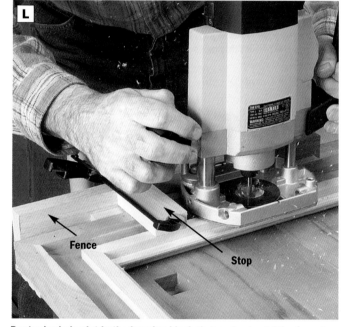

Fence

Stop

Rout a keyhole slot in the hanging block that ends about 9 in. from the top of the frame (see drawing).

on staining the cherry parts to increase the contrast between woods, you should do this before gluing the cove moldings.

To ensure the mirror would always hang straight and rest flat against the wall, I routed keyhole slots in the back with a hanging-slot bit. Glue the hanger blocks between the side coves and the side strips, centered about 9 in. from the top. Set up a fence and stop block **(see photo)** and cut the slot with a plunge router.

Keep your finishing simple. Good finishing options are Danish oil, wipe-on varnish or aerosol clear lacquer. Back the mirror with 1/8-in. hardboard before hanging.

Larry Okrend, *writer*
Scott Jacobson, *photos*
Gabriel Graphics, *illustration*

Wall Desk

Like most people, you're probably involved in an ongoing struggle against clutter. Modern life seems to be marked by piles of paper — junk mail, bills, fliers, newspapers, books, magazines and to-do lists. Of course, most of these items are important, and we need to keep them organized. This wall desk provides a place for you to begin that task. It is constructed out of solid mahogany, with a drop-down door that also functions as a writing surface. The actual writing surface is plastic laminate, which is smooth and easy to maintain, and provides an interesting color contrast with the mahogany frame.

Wall Desk

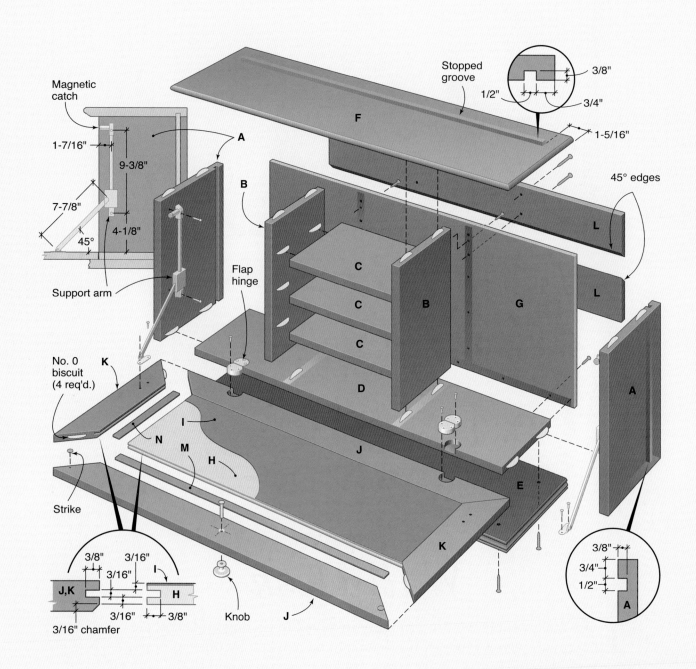

Magnetic catch

Stopped groove

3/8"

1/2"

3/4"

1-5/16"

45° edges

1-7/16"

9-3/8"

7-7/8"

4-1/8"

45°

Support arm

Flap hinge

No. 0 biscuit (4 req'd.)

Strike

3/8" 3/16"

3/16"

J,K   I   H

3/16"   3/8"

3/16" chamfer

Knob

A

B

B

C

C

C

D

E

F

G

H

I

J

J

K

K

K

L

L

M

N

A

3/8"

3/4"

1/2"

A

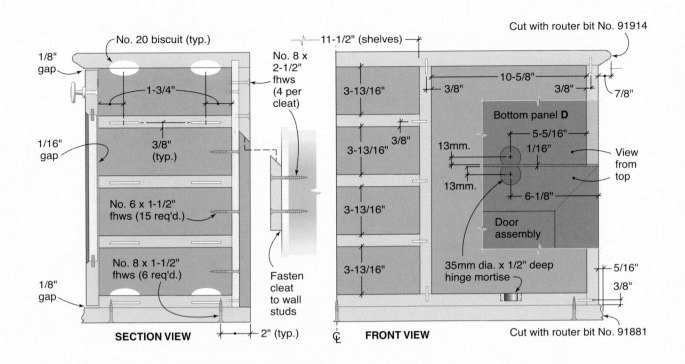

Cut with router bit No. 91914

No. 20 biscuit (typ.)

1/8" gap

1-3/4"

1/16" gap

3/8" (typ.)

No. 6 x 1-1/2" fhws (15 req'd.)

No. 8 x 1-1/2" fhws (6 req'd.)

1/8" gap

SECTION VIEW

2" (typ.)

No. 8 x 2-1/2" fhws (4 per cleat)

Fasten cleat to wall studs

11-1/2" (shelves)

3-13/16"

3-13/16"

3-13/16"

3-13/16"

3/8"

3/8"

10-5/8"

3/8"

3/8"

7/8"

Bottom panel **D**

5-5/16"

1/16"

13mm.

13mm.

6-1/8"

View from top

Door assembly

35mm dia. x 1/2" deep hinge mortise

5/16"

3/8"

FRONT VIEW

Cut with router bit No. 91881

Shopping List

- [ ] ½-in. mahogany plywood (¼ sheet)
- [ ] 8 bf ⁵⁄₄ mahogany (surfaced to 1 in.)
- [ ] 12 bf ⁴⁄₄ mahogany (surfaced to ¹³⁄₁₆ in.)
- [ ] 3 bf ⁴⁄₄ maple (surfaced to ¾ in.)
- [ ] 3 sf plastic laminate
- [ ] Fall-flap support arms; Rockler No. 30741 (2)
- [ ] Fall-flap hinges; Rockler No. 29447 (1 pair)
- [ ] Router bits: Rockler catalog No. 91914 and No. 91881
- [ ] Knob; Rockler No. 42852 (1)
- [ ] No. 6 x 1½-in. flathead wood screws
- [ ] No. 8 x 2½-in. flathead wood screws
- [ ] No. 8 x 1½-in. flathead wood screws
- [ ] No. 20 plate-joining biscuits
- [ ] No. 0 plate-joining biscuits
- [ ] Yellow glue
- [ ] Contact cement
- [ ] Transparent finish
- [ ] Brown mahogany wood stain

Materials and Cutting List

Part/Description		No.	Size
A	Sides	2	$^{13}/_{16} \times 10\frac{1}{2} \times 16$ in.
B	Inner partitions	2	$^{13}/_{16} \times 9 \times 15\frac{3}{16}$ in.
C	Shelves	3	$^{13}/_{16} \times 9 \times 11\frac{1}{2}$ in.
D	Inside bottom panel	1	$^{13}/_{16} \times 9 \times 34\frac{3}{8}$ in.
E	Bottom panel	1	$1 \times 11\frac{7}{16} \times 36\frac{5}{8}$ in.
F	Top	1	$1 \times 12 \times 37\frac{3}{4}$ in.
G	Back, plywood	1	$\frac{1}{2} \times 16\frac{3}{8} \times 35\frac{1}{8}$ in.
H	Door panel, plywood	1	$\frac{1}{2} \times 9\frac{3}{4} \times 30$ in.
I	Plastic-laminate panel	1	$^{1}/_{16} \times 10\frac{3}{4} \times 31$ in.**
J	Door rails	2	$^{13}/_{16} \times 3 \times 36$ in.
K	Door stiles	2	$^{13}/_{16} \times 3 \times 15\frac{3}{4}$ in.
L	Wall cleats, maple	2	$\frac{3}{4} \times 5 \times 34\frac{3}{8}$ in.
M	Spline	2	$^{3}/_{16} \times \frac{3}{4} \times 29$ in.
N	Spline	2	$^{3}/_{16} \times \frac{3}{4} \times 8\frac{3}{4}$ in.

*All parts mahogany except as noted
**Trim to finished size after laminating

GATHERING MATERIALS

I used $\frac{4}{4}$ and $\frac{5}{4}$ mahogany for the desk. Because mahogany is readily available in wide boards, you should not need to glue up panels for the wider case parts. If you choose another hardwood, you may have to assemble the panels for the top, bottom and sides from narrow stock.

The case back and door panels are ½-in. mahogany veneer on a medium-density fiberboard (MDF) core. I chose this core stock because it tends to be flatter and more stable than a veneer core. These panels are generally available from hardwood suppliers and some home centers. Because the project calls for only two small pieces, you might try to purchase a 4 × 4-ft. panel instead of the normal 4 × 8-ft. sheet.

If you don't own a jointer and planer, have your lumber supplier plane the $\frac{4}{4}$ stock to $\frac{13}{16}$ in. thick and the $\frac{5}{4}$ stock to 1 in. thick. You should insist that the stock be flat, without any cupping or warping in the boards, because it is almost impossible to build a high-quality piece of furniture with material that's not flat. You will also need a small amount of ¾-in.-thick maple stock for the wall cleats and splines.

CASE WORK

Begin by cutting all case parts to finished dimension. All joinery is done with plate-joining biscuits, so no allowances are needed for tenons.

Install the molding bit in the router table for shaping the case top profile. Although the bit has a ball-bearing pilot, clamp a fence to the table for safety's sake. Keep the leading edge of the fence flush with the bearing. Cut the profile on the panel ends first; then shape the front edge **(Photo A).** Change bits to shape the bottom panel.

Next, mark the biscuit slot locations in the case top, sides, shelves, partitions and inside bottom panel (see drawing). Use the plate joiner to cut the slots. When you need to cut slots in the face of a panel,

Shape the ends and front edge of the case top with a molding bit. Clamp a fence to the router table to help guide the workpiece.

When cutting biscuit slots in the center of a panel, clamp a straight-edge to the piece and position the plate joiner.

clamp a straightedge to the workpiece to help position the plate joiner **(Photo B).**

The case back rests in a groove cut in the case top and sides. Use a router with a spiral up-cutting bit and edge guide to make these cuts **(Photo C).** Notice that the groove in the case top stops short of the panel ends. Square the ends with a sharp chisel.

I used special fall-flap hinges for mounting the desk door. These hinges fit in a 35mm-dia. mortise cut in both the desk bottom and door. Clamp a fence to the drill press table to properly locate the holes. You'll need a 35mm bit to bore the mortises. (This size bit is commonly used to mount Euro-style hinges for cabinet construction, so if you need to purchase one, it will be a handy addition to your tool kit.) Lay out and bore the mortises in the case bottom **(Photo D);** then leave the drill press set up to bore the door mortises later.

Sand all interior surfaces of the case parts before you start assembling the case. This eliminates the need for awkward sanding in narrow spaces after assembly. Use 120-, 150-, and 220-grit sandpaper, dusting off thoroughly each time you change grits.

Once you've completed sanding, spread glue in the biscuit slots and on the biscuits for the partition-shelf joints **(Photo E).** Join the shelves to the partitions and clamp them to draw the joints tight. Compare opposite diagonal measurements to check that the assembly is square **(Photo F).** If necessary, adjust the clamps until the measurements are identical; then let the glue set before removing the clamps.

Next, join the partitions to the inside bottom panel; then add the case sides. When you clamp the sides, make sure that they stay square to the bottom **(Photo G).** When the glue sets, remove the clamps and add the case top.

C

Rout the grooves in the case back, top and sides using a spiral up-cutting bit. Mount an accessory edge guide on the router.

D

Clamp the fence to the drill press table; then bore the 35mm hinge recesses in the inside bottom panel.

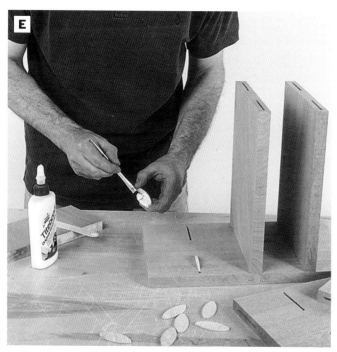

Begin case assembly by joining the shelves to the inner partitions. You can save time by sanding the parts before assembly.

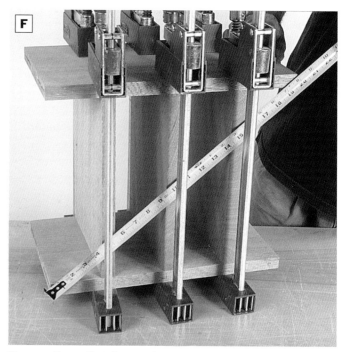

Measure diagonally to be sure that the assembly is square. Adjust clamping pressure to square the assembly.

Slide the case back into position in the side and top grooves. Drill and countersink pilot holes and screw the back to the partitions, shelves and bottom **(Photo H)**. Drill and countersink pilot holes in the bottom panel; then fasten it to the case.

Rip and cross-cut ¾-in.-thick maple stock to size for the wall cleats. Use the table saw to rip a 45-degree bevel along one long edge of each piece. Drill and countersink pilot holes in one of the strips for mounting it to the case back. Position the holes so the screws run into the edges of the partitions. Attach the cleat to the case. Note that the long point of the bevel should be positioned away from the back panel.

DOOR PARTS

After you've attached the cleat, begin making the door. Cut the door panel to size; then cut the plastic laminate about 1 in. longer and wider than the panel. You can use a jigsaw or band saw with a metal-cutting blade to cut the laminate. Next, coat the back of both the panel and laminate with water-based contact cement. Use a brush or roller to spread the cement, taking care to coat all surfaces evenly and completely. Allow the cement to dry until it doesn't feel sticky when you touch it.

To attach the laminate, first place a row of dowels across the door panel; then position the laminate over the dowels. The laminate should overhang the panel evenly on all edges **(Photo I)**. Start at one end and remove the dowels one at a time until the laminate

rests on the panel. Note that the cement grabs immediately, so adjusting the laminate is impossible. Use a small roller to press the laminate onto the panel. This works out any bubbles and ensures a good bond. Once the laminate is bonded to the panel, rout the overhang with a flush-trimming bit.

Next, place a ³⁄₁₆-in. slotting cutter in the router table and clamp a fence to the table to yield a ³⁄₈-in.-deep cut. With the laminate side down on the table, cut a slot in all edges of the door panel. To make the door frame, rip the stock for the door rails and stiles to width; then cut it to rough length. Readjust the height of the slotting cutter in the router table to cut a slot in the edges of the frame parts. Then install a chamfer bit in the router table to shape the molded edge of the frame parts. Cut 45-degree miters on the ends of the frame at the finished length. Lay out and cut biscuit slots in each mitered face.

Finally, cut splines to size for the door frame and panel and dry-assemble the parts to check the fit **(Photo J)**. If everything looks good, apply glue to the spline and biscuit joints and assemble the door. Use clamps to pull all joints tight; then let the glue set fully.

HARDWARE AND FINISHING

Once you've assembled the door, bore the door-hinge mortises; then attach the hinges to the case and the door. Engage the door hinges with those in the case **(Photo K)** and tighten the large screws that

G

Join the partition/shelf assembly to the inside bottom; then add the case sides. Be sure that the sides remain square to the bottom while the glue sets.

H

Slide the back panel into position. Drill and countersink pilot holes; then fasten the back to the shelves, bottom and partitions with flat-head screws.

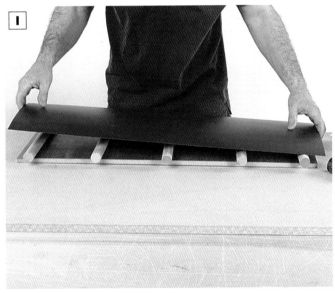

I

Spread contact cement on the door panel and plastic laminate. When the cement is dry to the touch, place dowels on the panel and position the laminate.

J

Cut splines about 1 in. shorter than panel dimensions; then carefully cut the door frame parts to size with 45-degree mitered ends.

hold the parts together. Use the small adjustment screws to level the door with the inside bottom panel. Attach the fall-flap supports to the case sides; then hold the door level to mark the pilot holes for the screws that attach the support arms **(Photo L).** Mount the strikes for the magnetic catches. Drill $\frac{1}{16}$-in.-dia. pilot holes for the strikes; then tap them in with a hammer. Finally, bore and counterbore a pilot hole for the knob, but don't mount it yet.

Finishing the case is easiest if you can break it down into component parts. To that end, remove the door and all hardware; then remove the bottom, wall cleat and case back. Sand all parts with 220-grit paper, and ease all edges as required.

I decided to stain the exterior of this case and leave the interior a natural mahogany color. Before staining, apply masking tape to the interior surfaces that abut the areas to be stained. Press the tape

Install the fall-flap hinges in both the case bottom and door. Engage the two parts of the hinge and lock them together with the large screw.

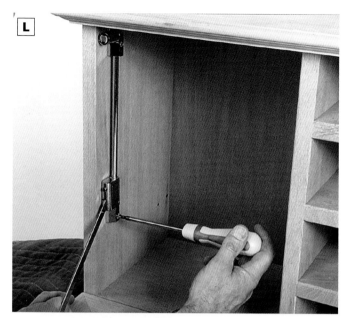

Attach the fall-flap supports to the case sides; then hold the lid in a horizontal position to mark to location of pilot holes for the support arm.

firmly onto the wood surface so the stain cannot bleed underneath. You should also mask the edges of the plastic-laminate writing surface so the finish won't stain the surface (**Photo M**).

I used a water-soluble brown mahogany stain, but use any stain that suits your design scheme. Water-soluble stains tend to raise the wood grain. To eliminate this problem, first lightly wipe the areas to be stained with a damp sponge. Then, when dry, lightly wipe the surface with 320-grit sandpaper to remove the raised grain. Do not sand too aggressively. Finally, apply the stain according to the manufacturer's directions.

When the stain is dry, you can apply the first coat of finish. (I used Waterlox Transparent Finish.) Use a brush or rag to coat the wood surface, allowing the finish to soak in for 20 to 30 minutes; then wipe off any excess. After overnight drying, lightly scuff the surface with 320-grit sandpaper and dust off. Apply two or three more coats, using the same technique. When the last coat is dry, you can buff the finish with 0000 steel wool and polish with a soft cloth.

INSTALLATION

Once the finishing is complete, assemble the case parts, including all hardware. To hang the desk on the wall, first locate the wall studs with an electronic stud finder. Transfer the stud location onto the wall cleat; then drill and countersink pilot holes for No. 8 × 2½-in. flathead screws. For a writing surface height of 29 in., mount the cleat to the wall with its bottom edge at a height of 35 in. The long point of

If you're staining only the outside of the case, apply masking tape to protect the areas adjacent to the stained surfaces. Also mask the plastic laminate.

the bevel should be held away from the wall surface. Make sure that the cleat is installed level. Finally, hang the desk on the wall, engaging the two beveled wall cleat edges.

Neal Barrett, *writer, photography*
Gabriel Graphics, *illustration*

Perfect Pair

The term European furniture conjures up visions of Old World craftsmen painstakingly making heirlooms you could pass on to your children. In reality, one of the most impressive factors is the design, especially the modular construction strategy of using similar-size components to make different pieces. With the benefits of modular construction in mind, we designed this bookcase and end table, which even a beginning woodworker can build. The pieces use the same stock and joinery, so you can complete both in about the time it takes to make just one.

Perfect Pair

END TABLE

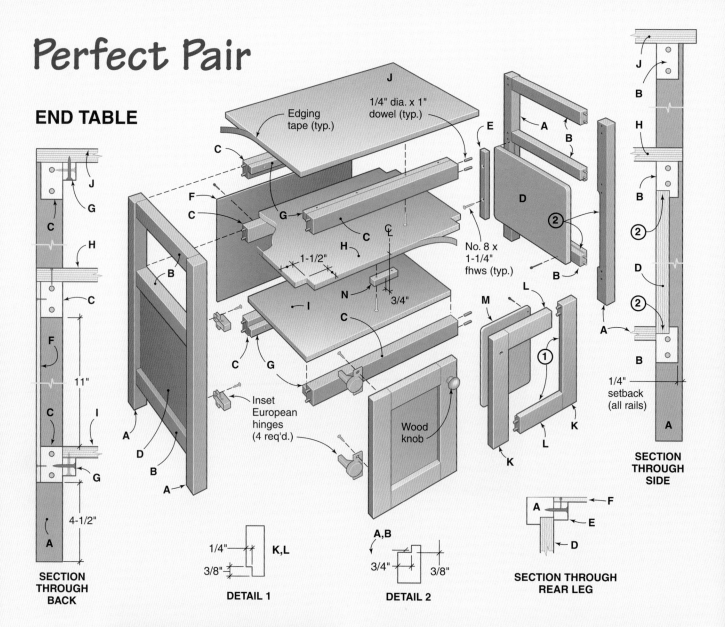

SECTION
THROUGH
BACK

DETAIL 1

K,L

1/4"

3/8"

DETAIL 2

A,B

3/4"   3/8"

SECTION THROUGH
REAR LEG

A
F
E
D

SECTION
THROUGH
SIDE

1/4"
setback
(all rails)

Inset
European
hinges
(4 req'd.)

Edging
tape (typ.)

1/4" dia. x 1"
dowel (typ.)

No. 8 x
1-1/4"
fhws (typ.)

Wood
knob

Inset
European
hinges
(4 req'd.)

Shopping List

- ☐ 1 × 4 × 8-ft. poplar boards (2)
- ☐ 1 × 6 × 8-ft. poplar boards (3)
- ☐ 1/4-in. × 2 × 4-ft. birch plywood
- ☐ 3/4-in. × 4 × 4-ft. birch plywood
- ☐ 1 3/16-in.-dia. wood knobs (2)
- ☐ Inset (Euro-style) cup hinges
- ☐ Birch plywood edging tape
- ☐ 1/4 × 1-in. dowels
- ☐ No. 8 × 1 1/4-in. wood screws
- ☐ 5/8-in. brad nails
- ☐ 1 1/4-in. finish nails

Materials and Cutting List

Part/Description	No.	Size
A Legs, poplar	4	$1\frac{1}{2} \times 1\frac{1}{2} \times 27\frac{1}{4}$ in.
B Side rails, poplar	6	$1\frac{1}{4} \times 2 \times 12\frac{1}{4}$ in.
C Front/back rails, poplar	5	$1\frac{1}{4} \times 2 \times 20\frac{1}{4}$ in.
D Side panels, birch plywood	2	$\frac{3}{4} \times 11\frac{3}{4} \times 13$ in.
E Back panel ledgers, poplar	2	$\frac{3}{4} \times 1 \times 11$ in.
F Back panel, birch plywood	1	$\frac{1}{4} \times 15 \times 20\frac{1}{4}$ in.
G Top and bottom ledgers, poplar	4	$\frac{3}{4} \times 1 \times 20\frac{1}{4}$ in.
H Shelf, birch plywood	1	$\frac{3}{4} \times 15\frac{1}{8} \times 23\frac{1}{8}$ in.
I Bottom, birch plywood	1	$\frac{3}{4} \times 12\frac{1}{4} \times 20\frac{1}{4}$ in.
J Top, birch plywood	1	$\frac{3}{4} \times 16 \times 24\frac{3}{4}$ in.
K Door stiles, poplar	4	$\frac{3}{4} \times 2 \times 13$ in.
L Door rails, poplar	4	$\frac{3}{4} \times 2 \times 6$ in.
M Door panels, birch plywood	2	$\frac{1}{4} \times 6\frac{5}{8} \times 9\frac{1}{2}$ in.
N Doorstop, poplar	1	$\frac{3}{4} \times 1 \times 3$ in.

BOOKCASE

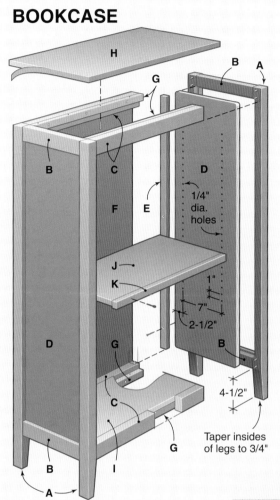

1/4" dia. holes

1"

7"

2-1/2"

4-1/2"

Taper insides of legs to 3/4"

Shopping List

☐ 1 × 4 × 8-ft. poplar boards (2)

☐ 1 × 6 × 8-ft. poplar boards (1)

☐ ¼-in. × 2 × 4-ft. birch plywood

☐ ³⁄₄-in. × 4 × 8-ft. birch plywood

☐ Birch plywood edging tape

☐ ¼ × 1-in. dowels

☐ No. 8 × 1¼-in. wood screws

☐ 1¼-in. finish nails

☐ ¼-in. shelf pins

Materials and Cutting List

Part/Description	No.	Size
A Legs, poplar	4	1½ × 1½ × 47¼ in.
B Side rails, poplar	4	1¼ × 2 × 10¼ in.
C Front/back rails, poplar	4	1¼ × 2 × 22¼ in.
D Side panels, birch plywood	2	³⁄₄ × 10⅞ × 38⅛ in.
E Back panel ledgers, poplar	2	³⁄₄ × 1 × 38½ in.
F Back panel, birch plywood	1	¼ × 22¼ × 42¼ in.
G Top and bottom ledgers, poplar	4	³⁄₄ × 1 × 22¼ in.
H Top, birch plywood	1	³⁄₄ × 14 × 27 in.
I Bottom, birch plywood	1	³⁄₄ × 10¼ × 22¼ in.
J Shelves, birch plywood	3	³⁄₄ × 11¼ × 22¼ in.
K Shelf edging, poplar	3	³⁄₄ × 1 × 22¼ in.

All of the materials can be found at a home center. If you already have a basic shop setup (table saw, router, drill/driver, etc.), the only specialty tools you'll need are a self-centering dowel jig and a 35mm Forstner bit.

Because the doors add a little more complexity, the following steps focus on how to build the end table. Any additional steps specific to the bookcase are addressed in "Build the Bookcase," p. 33.

MILL THE LEGS AND RAILS

The legs and rails for the end table and bookcase are made from 1× poplar that is face-glued to create 1½-in.-thick stock. Cut 1×4 poplar into four 28-in.-long pieces for the end table legs, and cut the 1×6 into six 35-in.-long pieces for the end table rails. Face-glue the pieces in pairs (**Photo A**).

When the glue has cured, rip the 1×4 leg stock to 1½ in. wide and the 1×6 rail stock to 2 in. wide; then rip the thickness to 1¼ in. Cut the legs and rails to

final length. Each 35-in. rail blank will yield one side rail and one front or back rail.

Using a self-centering dowel jig, drill ¼-in.-dia. × 1⅛-in.-deep dowel holes at all of the leg/rail connections. Center the dowels on the rails, and offset the dowel positions on the legs to keep the rails and posts flush on the inside of the case (**Photo B**).

MAKE THE TOP AND SHELVES

I used ¾-in. birch plywood for the top and shelves. The top shelf and bottom shelf are notched to fit around the legs.

Heat-activated wood edge banding conceals the edges that will be exposed, including all four edges of the top and the outside edges of the top shelf. Cut the banding 2 in. longer than the edge to be covered. Activate the banding with a household iron (**Photo C**). After the edge banding has cooled, trim the excess with a sharp chisel. (You can purchase a special trimmer designed for this purpose.) Lightly sand to ease any sharp edges.

A plywood top is easy to make, but it has drawbacks. The texture of the plywood core can telegraph through the surface veneer, especially if you apply a glossy finish. In addition, the veneer is very thin, making future repairs virtually impossible.

If you want to enhance the strength and appearance of the top, make it out of solid wood. Lumber-

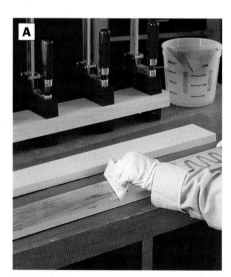

Apply polyurethane glue to one surface only. Spread the glue evenly over the part (legs are shown here), and use several clamps to ensure tight contact.

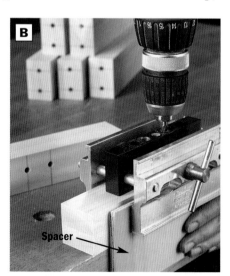

Spacer

Place a ¼-in.-thick spacer between the jig and the inside face of the leg to offset the dowel locations on the legs. The offset positions the rail flush with the inside of the leg.

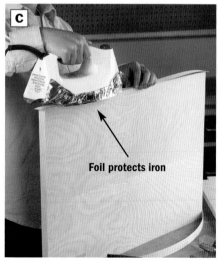

Foil protects iron

Press the edge banding down along each edge of the top and shelves, using an iron set on low heat. To ensure a good bond, follow the iron with a small roller while the edging is still warm.

Clamp the side frame with soft-face jaws or clamping pads to prevent marring. Check that the frame is square by measuring the diagonals.

Position the side frame on the workbench with the inside face up. Use a bearing-piloted rabbeting bit to cut the $\frac{3}{8} \times \frac{3}{4}$-in. rabbet in multiple passes.

yards may carry some varieties of preglued panel stock, but you will most likely have to edge-glue your own panel. You must attach any solid top with table-top fasteners or corner blocks with slotted screw holes. Both are designed to allow the wood to expand and contract as humidity changes.

ASSEMBLE THE CASE

Whether you're building the end table or the book-case, the case-assembly technique is the same: Start with the sides and build inward.

Apply glue to the dowels and assemble the sides, making sure they are square (**Photo D**). After the glue has cured, rout the $\frac{3}{8}$-in.-wide $\times$ $\frac{3}{4}$-in.-deep rab-bets for the side panels using a $\frac{3}{8}$-in.-dia. bearing-guided rabbeting bit (**Photo E**).

Cut the side panels to size, and trim the corners to fit inside the $\frac{3}{8}$-in.-radius corners of the rabbets. Apply glue in the rabbets and fasten the side panels with $1\frac{1}{4}$-in. brad nails. Solid panels must be able to expand and contract, but you can glue plywood pan-els in place. In fact, gluing provides reinforcement and prevents racking.

Next, connect the two side assemblies. Working with the case on its side, first glue the front and back rails into one side. Then fit the shelf in posi-tion and secure the other side assembly to the rails. The shelf must be installed at this stage because it will not fit into place later. After assembly you'll clamp the top shelf to the rails with glue and finish-ing nails.

Clamp the case parts together and then place the assembly upright on a flat surface. Adjust the clamps as necessary to square the case. Glue and fasten the back panel ledgers and back panel while the case-frame assembly is still clamped (**Photo F**).

Fasten the ledgers to the rails with $1\frac{1}{4}$-in. screws, and attach the bottom to the bottom ledgers with $1\frac{1}{4}$-in. screws. Do not attach the top until after you've applied the finish.

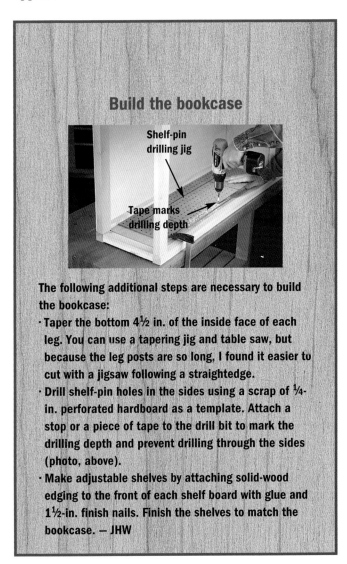

Build the bookcase

Shelf-pin drilling jig

Tape marks drilling depth

The following additional steps are necessary to build the bookcase:
- Taper the bottom $4\frac{1}{2}$ in. of the inside face of each leg. You can use a tapering jig and table saw, but because the leg posts are so long, I found it easier to cut with a jigsaw following a straightedge.
- Drill shelf-pin holes in the sides using a scrap of $\frac{1}{4}$-in. perforated hardboard as a template. Attach a stop or a piece of tape to the drill bit to mark the drilling depth and prevent drilling through the sides (photo, above).
- Make adjustable shelves by attaching solid-wood edging to the front of each shelf board with glue and $1\frac{1}{2}$-in. finish nails. Finish the shelves to match the bookcase. — JHW

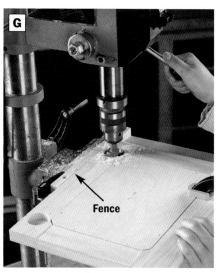

Fence

Connect the two side frames and remaining rails with the top shelf in place. Glue and fasten the back panel with 1¼-in. finishing nails while the case is still clamped to keep it square.

Drill a 35mm (or 1⅜-in.-dia.) mortise for the cup hinges. Clamp a fence to position the center of the bit at the specified distance from the edge of the door. Mark a bit center-line on the top of the fence and a hole center-line on the door.

Fasten the hinge to the door and the mounting bracket to the cabinet (inset photo). Slide the hinge arm onto the mounting bracket, and center the door in the cabinet opening using the adjustment screws.

MAKE AND HANG THE DOORS

Measure the opening and cut the door stiles and rails to fit. Like the side panels, the door panels fit into a rabbet.

Assemble the door stiles and rails with dowels, making sure the frames are square. After the glue has cured, rout a ⅜-in.-wide × ¼-in.-deep rabbet around the inside edge of each door frame. Glue and fasten the panels in the rabbets with ⅝-in. brad nails.

I used flush-hanging cup hinges (Euro-style) to hang the door. These hinges are easy to adjust and remove. Use a 35mm bit and drill press to bore the hinge cup mortises in the doors (**Photo G**). Screw the hinges to the door, and attach the mounting clips to the cabinet. Snap the doors into place, and center them using the built-in hinge-adjustment screws (**Photo H**).

Center and fasten the doorstop to the bottom of the top shelf with 1¼-in. screws. Drill ³⁄₁₆-in.-dia. holes at each doorknob location.

FINISH THE PARTS

You can use paint or stain and polyurethane to finish the table. I decided to leave the top natural and paint the case and shelves.

Sand the top with increasingly finer grades of sandpaper (ending with 220-grit). I applied a first coat of oil-base polyurethane diluted 50/50 with mineral spirits. After the first coat dried, I lightly sanded with 320-grit paper. Then I applied two additional coats of undiluted polyurethane, sanding lightly between coats.

The quality of the paint job can make or break a furniture project. I chose water-base enamel designed for furniture, but you can use oil or latex interior trim paint instead. To achieve the best finish, follow these tips:

- Hold a light at a low angle to look for major scratches or dents. Fill deep blemishes with wood putty, and sand the entire piece with 150-grit sandpaper. The paint will cover any swirl marks.
- Apply primer to block stains and seal the wood so it will evenly receive a topcoat. If you are using a dark-color paint, ask the paint supplier to tint the primer for easier coverage.
- When using latex paint, mix it with Flood Floetrol, an additive that extends the open time and makes the paint flow more like oil-base enamel.
- Brush the corners and seams first and then use a ¼-in.-nap or foam roller to cover the large areas. Start with the inside faces and move to the outside, covering one side entirely before moving on to the next.
- Give your project an extra day to dry before attaching the top and placing it on carpet. Even when latex paint appears to be dry, it may still be sticky. (You can probably guess how I learned this.)

Joe Hurst-Wajszczuk, *writer*
Mark Macemon, *photography*
Gabriel Graphics, *illustrations*

Scenic Storage

Many older homes feature built-in window seats that provide storage as well as a place to enjoy the view. To recapture this architectural spirit in a modern home, we designed a window bench that doesn't require additional interior walls. Treat it as a piece of furniture or attach it to the floor as a permanent structure. At its core is a simple case or chest with two drawers. We embellished this chest with arms and a base to create a bench-style seat. Adapt surroundings with simple modifications to the arm or base styling.

Scenic Storage

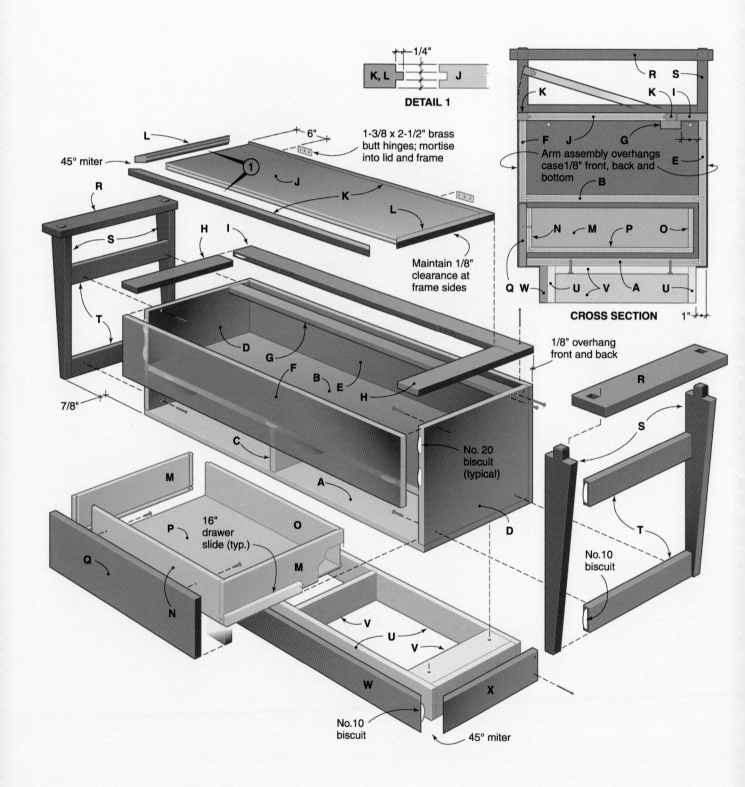

1/4"

K, L   J

DETAIL 1

L

45° miter

R

S

6"

1-3/8 x 2-1/2" brass butt hinges; mortise into lid and frame

J

K

L

Maintain 1/8" clearance at frame sides

H   I

R

S

T

7/8"

D

G

F

B   E

C

H

A

No. 20 biscuit (typical)

D

M

P   16" drawer slide (typ.)   O

Q

M

N

V

U

V

W

X

No.10 biscuit

45° miter

R   S

K   K   I

F   J   G

Arm assembly overhangs case1/8" front, back and bottom

E

B

N   M   P   O

Q   W   U   V   A   U

CROSS SECTION

1"

1/8" overhang front and back

R

S

T

No.10 biscuit

Case Cutting List

Part/Description	No.	Size
A Bottom, birch plywood	1	$3/4 \times 16\frac{1}{2} \times 48$ in.
B False bottom, cherry plywood	1	$3/4 \times 16\frac{1}{2} \times 46\frac{1}{2}$ in.
C Drawer divider, birch plywood	1	$3/4 \times 5\frac{1}{4} \times 16\frac{1}{2}$ in.
D Sides, cherry plywood	2	$3/4 \times 13 \times 16\frac{1}{2}$ in.
E Back, cherry plywood	1	$3/4 \times 13 \times 48$ in.
F Front, cherry plywood	1	$3/4 \times 7\frac{3}{4} \times 48$ in.
G Lid support, cherry	1	$3/4 \times 2 \times 46\frac{1}{2}$ in.
H Lid frame sides, cherry	2	$3/4 \times 3 \times 15\frac{1}{4}$ in.
I Lid frame back, cherry	1	$3/4 \times 3 \times 48$ in.
J Lid, cherry plywood	1	$3/4 \times 13\frac{1}{4} \times 39\frac{3}{4}$ in.
K Lid edge front/back, cherry	2	$3/4 \times 1\frac{1}{4} \times 41\frac{3}{4}$ in.
L Lid edge sides, cherry	2	$3/4 \times 1\frac{1}{4} \times 15\frac{1}{8}$ in.

Drawers Cutting List

Part/Description	No.	Size
M Drawer sides, birch plywood	2	$1/2 \times 4\frac{3}{8} \times 16$ in.
N Drawer front, birch plywood	1	$1/2 \times 4\frac{3}{8} \times 21\frac{1}{4}$ in.
O Drawer back, birch plywood	1	$1/2 \times 3\frac{7}{8} \times 21\frac{1}{4}$ in.
P Drawer bottom, birch plywood	1	$1/2 \times 15\frac{3}{4} \times 21\frac{1}{4}$ in.
Q Drawer faces, cherry	2	$3/4 \times 5\frac{7}{8} \times 23\frac{3}{4}$ in.

Arms Cutting List

Part/Description	No.	Size
R Armrests, cherry	2	$1 \times 4 \times 19\frac{1}{2}$ in.
S Arm supports, cherry	4	$1 \times 3 \times 20\frac{3}{4}$ in.
T Arm crosspieces, cherry	4	$1 \times 2\frac{1}{2} \times 16\frac{1}{8}$ in.

Base Cutting List

Part/Description	No.	Size
U Base front/back, pine	2	$3/4 \times 3\frac{1}{2} \times 44\frac{1}{2}$ in.
V Base crosspieces, pine	5	$3/4 \times 3\frac{1}{2} \times 12\frac{3}{4}$ in.
W Base skirt front, cherry	1	$3/4 \times 3\frac{1}{2} \times 46$ in.
X Base skirt sides, cherry	2	$3/4 \times 3\frac{1}{2} \times 15$ in.

Shopping List

- ☐ 10 bf $5/4$ cherry
- ☐ 20 bf $4/4$ cherry
- ☐ 1 $4 \times 8\frac{3}{4}$-in. cherry-veneer plywood
- ☐ 1 $2 \times 4\frac{3}{4}$-in. birch plywood
- ☐ 1 $5 \times 5\frac{1}{2}$-in. Baltic birch plywood
- ☐ (2) $2\frac{1}{2} \times 1\frac{3}{8}$-in. brass butt hinges
- ☐ 2 pairs 16-in. drawer slides
- ☐ No. 20 biscuits
- ☐ No. 10 biscuits
- ☐ Yellow glue
- ☐ No. 8×2-in. wood screws
- ☐ No. $8 \times 1\frac{1}{4}$-in. wood screws
- ☐ No. 8×1-in. wood screws
- ☐ $1\frac{1}{4}$-in. finish nails

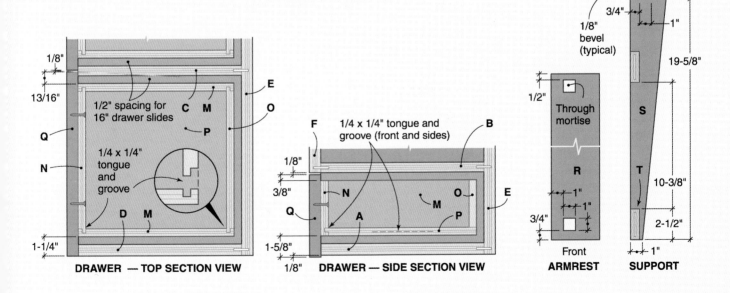

DRAWER — TOP SECTION VIEW

DRAWER — SIDE SECTION VIEW

ARMREST

SUPPORT

MATERIAL PREPARATION

All of the visible parts for the case can be cut from one sheet of hardwood-veneer plywood — I chose cherry. To avoid purchasing another full sheet for the remaining interior parts, I used a 2 × 4-ft. piece of ¾-in. birch plywood, sometimes called a "handy panel," available at most home centers.

Before assembling the case, you'll need to finish a few edges that will be exposed. Attach solid ⅛-in. edging or apply heat-activated veneer edge tape to the front edges of the drawer divider and bottom. Also apply edging to the bottom 5¼ in. of the front edges of the sides and to the top and bottom edge of the front. Trim the edges flush with a low-angle block plane and cabinet scraper.

THE CASE PARTS

Assemble the case using butt joints reinforced with No. 20 biscuits **(Photos A and B).** After you've fastened the case panels together, install the lid support between the two sides with glue and No. 8 × 2-in. wood screws.

The lid frame rests on the sides and back of the case and is made of solid cherry milled to match the thickness of the plywood, about ¾ in. Assemble the lid frame with glue and biscuits and check that it is square.

The lid is made of plywood for stability and is wrapped with solid-wood edging to give it durability. The edging connects to the plywood with tongue-and-groove joints and is mitered at the corners.

When making tongue-and-groove joints, I prefer to start with the groove and then cut the tongue to fit. I chose to cut the groove with a table saw and dado set, centering a ¼-in.-wide × ¼-in.-deep groove on all four edges of the plywood **(Photo C).**

Create the tongue by cutting rabbets along the top and bottom inside edges of the edging stock. I again used the dado set to cut these rabbets. To ensure that the edge pieces align properly around the lid, you'll

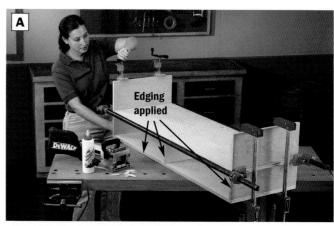

Begin the case asssembly by gluing the drawer divider between the bottom and interior bottom. Next, glue the sides to the bottoms.

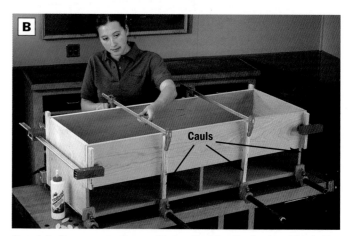

Complete the case panel assembly by attaching the front and back. To achieve even clamping pressure on the front use cauls that extend below the front panel.

need to cut the tongue in the entire length of edge stock before cutting each piece to length.

Adjust the dado set to a ⅜-in. thickness and attach a sacrificial fence to your saw's rip fence. Lower the blade below the table and then slide the fence in so that ⅛ in. of the blade is under the fence. Start the saw and gradually raise the blade to just under ¼ in. The blade will cut into the sacrificial fence as you raise it.

Use a scrap to test the setup. Run the piece through twice, flipping it so that the edge features mirrored rabbets. Test the fit of the tongue in the plywood groove. If the tongue is too wide, raise the blade slightly, repeat the cuts and check the fit again. If it is too narrow, lower the blade and make new test cuts. Once you get a snug fit, use that setup to cut the actual edge stock **(Photo D).**

Cut the edge pieces to length, mitering the ends of each piece 45 degrees. Cut each piece slightly long, check the fit and trim as needed.

Glue and clamp the edge pieces to the lid **(Photo E).**

It is easier to cut the hinge mortises before attaching the lid frame to the case. Position the hinges so that only the top half of the hinge barrel is exposed above the surface of the lid.

I used a router to cut the hinge mortises. Mount the hinges and check the lid operation.

You can remove the lid and hinges from the case until after you've applied the finish. Now apply glue to the top of the case sides and back as well as to the top of the lid support. Clamp the lid frame in position and secure with 1¼-in. finish nails **(Photo F).**

THE DRAWERS

The drawers are made of ½-in. Baltic birch plywood, which provides excellent strength and stability and an attractive, void-free nine-ply edge grain. The drawer features rabbet-and-dado joints, allowing you to use a ¼-in. dado setup for all of the cuts.

Begin by cutting all of the ¼ × ¼-in. dadoes in the drawer parts. Cut dadoes along the front and back edges and along the bottom of the sides. Also cut a dado along the bottom of the inside of the front.

Next, cut the corresponding ¼ × ¼-in. rabbets. Cut rabbets along each side of the fronts and backs. Also cut rabbets along the sides and front of the bottom.

Glue and clamp the drawer boxes together, and check that they are square **(Photo G).**

Install the drawer slides and drawer boxes in the drawer openings. When you are satisfied with their operation, attach the drawer faces.

THE ARMS

The solid-cherry arm assemblies feature through-tenons. Mill the stock for the armrests and arm supports to 1-in. thickness and the stock for the cross-pieces to ¾ in. Cut all arm pieces to rough size. Wait to cut the tapers in the arm supports until after you've made the tenons.

Use a ¼-in. dado setup to cut the grooves in the lid. Attach a sacrificial fence to the saw's rip fence to help support the lid in the vertical position.

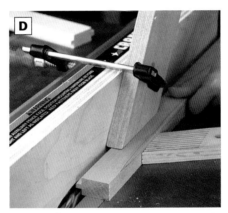

Raise the ⅜-in. dado blade up into the sacrificial fence approximately ⅛ in. Run test pieces through to get the proper tongue size; then cut the actual edging.

Glue and clamp the edging to the lid using cauls to distribute the pressure.

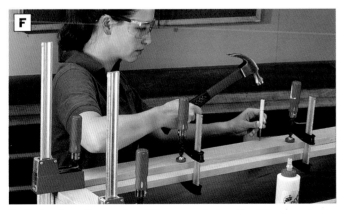

Apply glue along the top edge of the case and where the lid frame rests on the top of the lid support. Clamp the lid frame to the case and drive 1¼-in. finish nails through the frame and into the back and sides of the case.

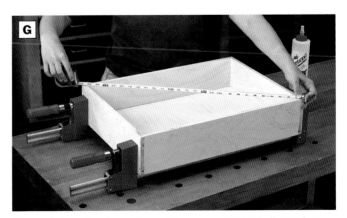

Glue and clamp the drawer boxes. Measure across each diagonal to check for square. If the measurements across the diagonals are the same, then the box is square.

Cut tapers in the arm supports using a tapering jig. You can make your own tapering jig or use a purchased jig. Use a pushstick as a hold-down. NOTE: The blade guard and splitter were removed for photo clarity.

Dry-fit (no glue) the armrests to the arm supports before gluing to be sure the tenons fit well in the mortises.

Attach the arm assemblies to the case with glue and No. 8 × 1¼-in. screws. Drill pilot holes and drive the screws through the inside of the case.

Attach the base frame to the bottom of the case with 1¼-in. screws.

When creating mortise-and-tenon joints, always cut the mortise first and then cut the tenon to fit. The position of the mortises is critical. Be sure to leave at least ½ in. of stock for the back mortise wall to prevent it from breaking out. Clamp the crosspieces between the arm supports and hold the armrest against the supports to locate the mortises. Drill out the center of the mortises using a 1-in. Forstner bit. Then square off the mortises with a chisel.

Each tenon should be ⅛ in. longer than the thickness of the armrest so that it will extend slightly above the top of the armrest. Lay out and cut each tenon slightly thicker than its final size. I used a band saw to make these cuts, but you could use a backsaw or table saw.

Check the fit of the tenons; then shave them to size with a plane, chisel or file. The tenons should fit snugly but not too tightly. If they are too large, they could split the wood.

After cutting the tenons in each arm support, taper the outside edges of each support on the table saw using an adjustable tapering jig (**Photo H**). Each should taper from 3 in. at the top to 1 in. at the bottom.

Assemble the crosspieces and arm supports using glue and No. 10 biscuits. With clamps in place, apply glue to the tenons and tap the armrests onto the arm supports (**Photo I**). Shim the case so that the bottom of the arms are ⅛-in. below the bottom of the case. Finally, fasten the arm assemblies to the case with glue and No. 8 × 1¼-in. screws (**Photo J**).

THE BASE

The base is simply a 1×4 pine frame that will be concealed by solid wood or base molding to match the room where you'll install the bench. Assemble the frame with glue and No. 20 biscuits. Position the frame 1 in. from the back and center it between the sides. Attach it with No. 8 × 1¼-in. screws (**Photo K**).

Because I wanted to treat the bench as a movable piece of furniture, I wrapped the front and sides of the base with solid ¾ cherry stock. I glued the miters and attached the base trim with 1¼-in. finish nails. I then finished the project with a few coats of wipe-on poly/oil-blend finish, rubbing out the finish with 0000 steel wool between coats.

If you prefer a built-in approach, wait to attach the base trim until after the installation. Position the bench and level it with shims. Toe-screw through the base frame and shims into the floor. Then finish the trim and scribe it to follow the contours of the floor.

Dan Cary, *writer*
Mark Macemon, *photography*
Gabriel Graphics, *illustration*

Classic Accent Table

I f you have some holiday gift requests to fill, this accent table is
a quick and elegant project that's sure to please even the most
discriminating recipient. Its clean, classic lines will complement
almost any decor, and it can turn an unused hallway space or the
area behind a sofa into an attractive focal point for collectibles. The
project also provides a good opportunity to practice your joint-making
skills, and you can complete it in a couple of long afternoons.

Classic Accent Table

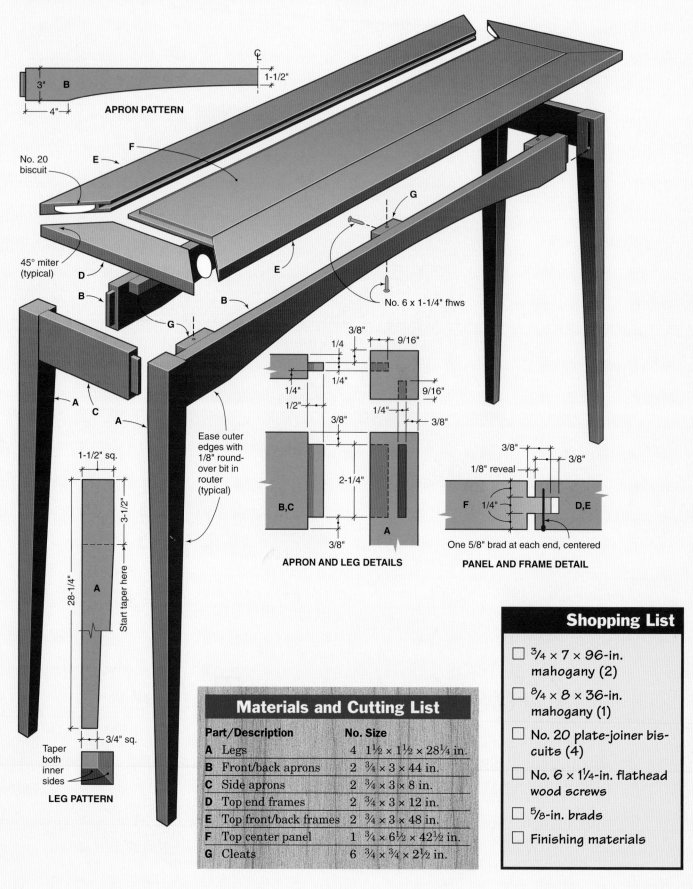

1-1/2"

3" B

4"

APRON PATTERN

No. 20 biscuit

E

F

45° miter (typical)

D

B

B

G

G

A

C

A

A

No. 6 x 1-1/4" fhws

Ease outer edges with 1/8" round-over bit in router (typical)

1-1/2" sq.

3-1/2"

28-1/4"

Start taper here

A

3/4" sq.

Taper both inner sides

LEG PATTERN

3/8"

1/4

9/16"

1/4"

1/4"

1/4"

1/2"

3/8"

9/16"

3/8"

3/8"

2-1/4"

1/4"

B,C

A

3/8"

APRON AND LEG DETAILS

3/8"

3/8"

1/8" reveal

F

1/4"

D,E

One 5/8" brad at each end, centered

PANEL AND FRAME DETAIL

Materials and Cutting List

Part/Description	No.	Size
A Legs	4	$1\frac{1}{2} \times 1\frac{1}{2} \times 28\frac{1}{4}$ in.
B Front/back aprons	2	$\frac{3}{4} \times 3 \times 44$ in.
C Side aprons	2	$\frac{3}{4} \times 3 \times 8$ in.
D Top end frames	2	$\frac{3}{4} \times 3 \times 12$ in.
E Top front/back frames	2	$\frac{3}{4} \times 3 \times 48$ in.
F Top center panel	1	$\frac{3}{4} \times 6\frac{1}{2} \times 42\frac{1}{2}$ in.
G Cleats	6	$\frac{3}{4} \times \frac{3}{4} \times 2\frac{1}{2}$ in.

Shopping List

- ☐ $\frac{3}{4} \times 7 \times 96$-in. mahogany (2)
- ☐ $\frac{8}{4} \times 8 \times 36$-in. mahogany (1)
- ☐ No. 20 plate-joiner biscuits (4)
- ☐ No. 6 × $1\frac{1}{4}$-in. flathead wood screws
- ☐ $\frac{5}{8}$-in. brads
- ☐ Finishing materials

Most of the project can be made from ¾-in. lumber, but buy thicker ⁸/₄ stock for the legs so you won't have to glue together two thinner boards — glue seams and irregular grain patterns on the legs can be distracting.

The tapered legs and gentle curves of the aprons give the table a sophisticated and graceful stature, so choose top-quality lumber to build it. I used mahogany, but cherry, walnut or maple would also be good choices. A piece of figured wood can add visual interest to the center panel of the tabletop if the other parts are made of plain-grain stock. You can even make the center panel from a contrasting wood species for a more contemporary look.

MAKE THE LEGS

To begin, joint and plane the leg stock to uniform thickness (1½ in.), and rip the four leg blanks slightly larger than necessary. On each leg, run one of the sawn faces over the jointer to smooth it; then plane the other sawn face to reduce the leg to its final dimensions. Cross-cut the legs to length.

It may be tempting to cut the leg tapers next, but instead you should cut mortises for the apron tenons while the leg faces are still flat. Lay out the mortise positions carefully. Notice in the drawing that the

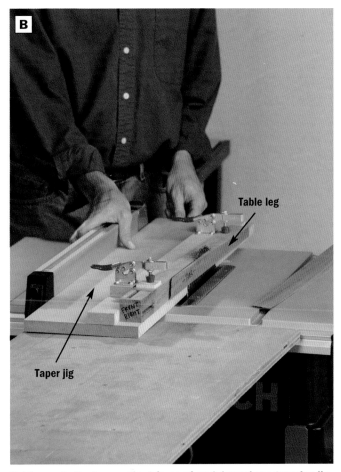

A

Cut ½-in.-deep mortises in the legs for the apron tenons. A mortising machine or a router table and straight bit will cut the mortises efficiently.

Machine mortising chisel

B

Table leg

Taper jig

Cut tapers in the two mortised faces of each leg using a tapering jig on a table saw. Slide the jig along the rip fence to make these angled cuts.

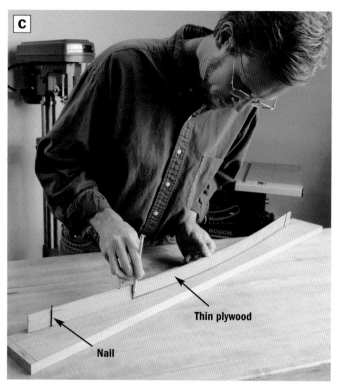

Nail

Thin plywood

Draw the long apron curves by flexing a strip of thin plywood or hardboard between two nails. Gang-cut both curves with the aprons taped together.

Dado blade

Use a dado blade in a table saw to cut tenons on the ends of the aprons. Set the rip fence to index the tenon shoulder cuts.

location of the mortises creates an attractive ⅛-in. setback where the legs meet the aprons.

A mortising machine and ¼-in. hollow-chisel bit will cut the leg mortises quickly. You can also use a ¼-in. straight bit mounted in a router table if you don't have a mortising machine (or a drill press mortising attachment). Plunge the leg down onto the router bit and slide it along the fence to cut the mortises (**Photo A**).

If you rout the mortises, make them in a series of three or four passes, raising the bit in ⅛-in. increments for each pass. Chisel the ends of the mortises square.

Once you've completed the mortises, cut tapers along the mortised faces (**Photo B**). I cut the tapers on a table saw using a shop-made tapering jig with a pair of hold-down clamps, but you could use a commercial jig instead. Adjust the jig and saw fence settings so the tapers start 3½ in. from the tops of the legs and reduce the legs to ¾ in. at the bottom. Double-check the leg orientation before you make these cuts to avoid mistakes.

After you've cut the tapers, joint the angled faces smooth. Finish the legs by easing all sharp edges.

PREPARE THE APRONS

Rip and cross-cut the short side aprons to final size, but rip the long front and back aprons about 1

in. oversize. This extra material gives you room to lay out the bottom curves. Mark the aprons to their 3-in. width and plot the end and center points of the broad curve. Scribe the curve by flexing a strip of thin plywood or hardboard between two finish nails driven into the end points of the curve (in the apron waste area). Rip the long aprons to final width, but don't cut the curves yet (**Photo C**).

The tenons on all four aprons match, so you can machine them consecutively with a wide dado blade on the table saw. Set the saw's rip fence so the blade reaches the tenon shoulders, and use the miter gauge to support the workpieces from behind while you cut the tenons. (Test the setup on a scrap first.) After you've cut away the initial waste for all eight tenons, raise the dado blade to make the deeper end shoulder cuts — they're ⅜ in. deep, not ¼ in. like the others (**Photo D**).

Now you can cut the long apron curves. Hold the aprons together with a strip of double-sided carpet tape, and cut both curves at once with a jigsaw or band saw. Sand the curves smooth.

Sand the legs and aprons to 180-grit, and test the fit of the tenons in the mortises. The parts should slide together without force. If you need to improve the fit, use a file or sharp chisel to adjust the tenon proportions a little at a time. Then glue and clamp the legs and aprons together to create the lower framework. Make the six inner cleats for attaching

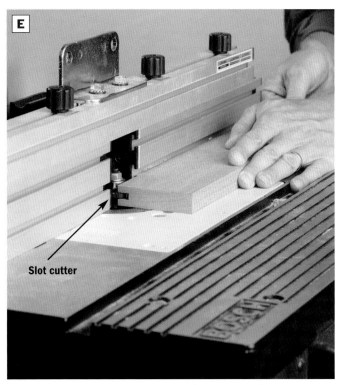

Mill a centered groove along the edges of the tabletop frame workpieces with a slot-cutting bit mounted in a router table.

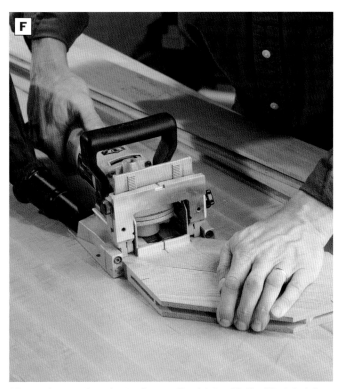

Align and strengthen the top frame miter joints with No. 20 plate-joining biscuits. Cut the slots with a plate joiner.

the top, and fasten them to the aprons with glue and countersunk No. 6 × 1¼-in. flathead wood screws.

BUILD THE TOP FRAME

The tabletop is essentially a mitered frame-and-panel assembly similar to a cabinet door. A groove around the inside of the frame houses a tongue on the center panel. The panel is intentionally undersize in width and length to allow for wood movement and create a ⅛-in. decorative reveal inside the frame.

Make the tabletop by first ripping and crosscutting the short and long frame members to size. Joint the long edges of these parts smooth. Next, cut a centered ¼-in.-wide × ⅜-in.-deep groove along one edge of the four frame parts for the center panel. You can make the grooves on a router table using either a slot-cutting or straight bit, or you can cut them with a dado blade in a table saw. An easy way to ensure that each groove is centered is to make it in two passes, flipping the workpiece from one face to the other before making the second pass **(Photo E).**

Once you've milled all of the grooves, carefully cut the frame end miters to 45 degrees. (Test the saw's angle setting by first cutting a scrap.) Be sure the lengths of the short and long frame parts match after you cut the angles. Use a plate joiner to make centered slots in the ends for installing a single No. 20 plate-joiner biscuit across each miter joint **(Photo F).**

Mill a centered tongue around the edges of the tabletop center panel with a router and piloted rabbeting bit.

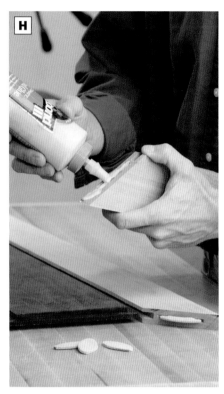

Apply finish to the center panel, then glue the tabletop biscuit joints. Keep glue out of the grooves so the panel is free to expand and contract.

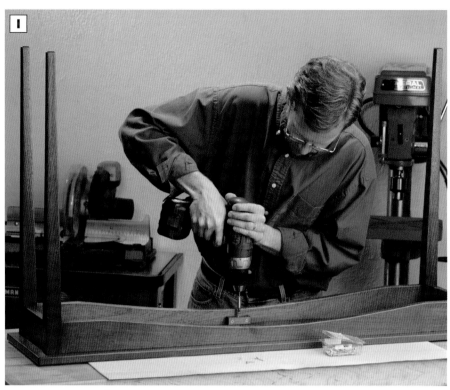

Drive a countersunk 1¼-in. flathead wood screw through each cleat to attach the lower frame to the tabletop.

If you don't have a plate joiner, you can use dowels or splines. Sand the frame parts smooth.

MAKE THE CENTER PANEL

Cut the center panel to size, and use a rabbeting bit mounted in a handheld router to mill the centered tongue around all four edges of the panel **(Photo G).** Rout all around one face; then flip the panel and rout the other face to create each tongue. (Check the bit settings first on a scrap.) The tongue should fit easily but not sloppily into the frame grooves.

Sand the panel thoroughly, and apply finish before assembling the frame. This way if the panel shrinks because of changes in humidity, bare wood won't be exposed in the reveal area.

ASSEMBLE AND FINISH

Slip the center panel into the frame grooves and spread glue carefully into the biscuit slots and along the mitered ends. Keep the glue out of the center panel groove so the panel will float freely after assembly **(Photo H).** Insert the biscuits and use a strap clamp to pull the assembly together.

After the glue dries, adjust the panel in the frame so the reveal is even on all sides. To keep the panel from slipping out of position, drive a single

⅝-in. brad through the short frame pieces (centered and from the bottom) where the tongue and grooves overlap.

Complete the tabletop's construction by easing the outer edges with a ⅛-in. roundover bit mounted in a router; then sand the edges before finishing. I used a mixture of water-base brown and red aniline dye to evenly stain the mahogany and then applied a coat of dewaxed shellac to seal the piece and enhance the wood grain and color. For improved durability, you can apply several coats of oil-base varnish over the shellac. If you're working on a tight deadline, however, you can simply use conventional wood stain and varnish.

Once the finish has cured, all that's left is to join the leg assembly to the tabletop. Drive six countersunk No. 6 × 1¼-in. flathead wood screws through the cleats and up into the tabletop frame, and your gift is ready to wrap **(Photo I).**

Chris Marshall, *writer*
Alan Geho, *photography*
Gabriel Graphics, *illustration*

Compact Cook's Rack

Many people assume that creating curved wood pieces takes a lot of time and requires an elaborate steaming contraption, but that's not true. Using a simple method called bentwood lamination, you can make precise, strong, stable curves in your shop. Use bentwood lamination to build this cook's rack — for about $75 in materials — which rivals racks costing much more. The process involves gluing thin strips of wood together in a press that is shaped like the curve you wish to achieve. we used cherry, but you could use just about any solid wood. The project should take one weekend. (For more information on bentwood lamination, see "Finer Futon Frame," page 70.)

Compact Cook's Rack

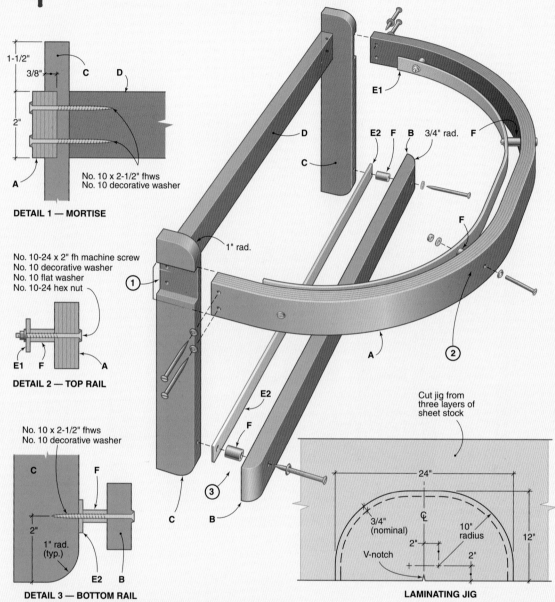

DETAIL 1 — MORTISE

1-1/2"
3/8"
C
D
2"
A

No. 10 x 2-1/2" fhws
No. 10 decorative washer

DETAIL 2 — TOP RAIL

No. 10-24 x 2" fh machine screw
No. 10 decorative washer
No. 10 flat washer
No. 10-24 hex nut

E1 F A

DETAIL 3 — BOTTOM RAIL

No. 10 x 2-1/2" fhws
No. 10 decorative washer

C F
2"
1" rad. (typ.)
E2 B

E1
D
C
E2 F B 3/4" rad. F
1" rad.
F
A
1
2
E2
F
3
C
B

Cut jig from three layers of sheet stock

LAMINATING JIG

24"
3/4" (nominal)
10" radius
2"
2"
12"
V-notch

Shopping List

- ☐ 6 bf ³/₄-in. cherry or two 1 × 6 × 8-ft. boards
- ☐ ¹/₈ × 1-in. × 6-ft. aluminum strip
- ☐ ¹/₂-in.-dia. × 6-in. aluminum tubing
- ☐ No. 10 × 2-in. flathead slotted machine screws (4)
- ☐ No. 10 × 2¹/₂-in. flathead slotted wood screws (6)
- ☐ No. 10 decorative washers (10)
- ☐ No. 10 flat-cut washers (4)
- ☐ No. 10 nuts (4)

Materials and Cutting List

Part/Description		No.	Size
A	Top rack strips	6	¹/₈ × 2 × 48 in.*
B	Bottom rack	1	³/₄ × 2 × 26¹/₄ in.
C	Sides	2	³/₄ × 2 × 14¹/₂ in.
D	Wall brace	1	³/₄ × 2 × 22¹/₂ in.
E1	Top aluminum rail	1	¹/₈ × 1 × 36 in.**
E2	Bottom aluminum rail	1	¹/₈ × 1 × 24 in.
F	Tubing spacers	6	¹/₂ in. dia. × ³/₄ in.

All wood parts are cherry.
*Length before lamination
**Length before bending and cutting to fit

Compact Cook's Rack: Instructions

More than half of the work required to build this project goes into making the laminating jig, which must be sturdy and stable. I built this one out of a sheet material called Woodstalk fiberboard, a lighter-weight alternative to particleboard.

To begin, cut a ¾-in. × 4 × 8-ft. panel into four 18 × 36-in. pieces. Transfer the curve pattern (see diagram, p. 48) to one of the pieces of jig material. I made a compass out of a thin scrap to draw the 10-in. radii on the layout (**Photo A**).

Stack, clamp and screw together three pieces of the jig material. The piece with the layout drawing should be on top. Keep all screws clear of the curve. Cut out the curve using a jigsaw or band saw.

Cutting through thick stacks like this can make a band saw or jigsaw blade pull out of vertical alignment.

To lessen this problem (called blade deflection), move slowly along the cut line, using a blade with a low tooth count (5 to 8 tpi). Another method is to cut inside the line by ⅛ in. and sand back to the line using a drum sander or oscillating spindle sander.

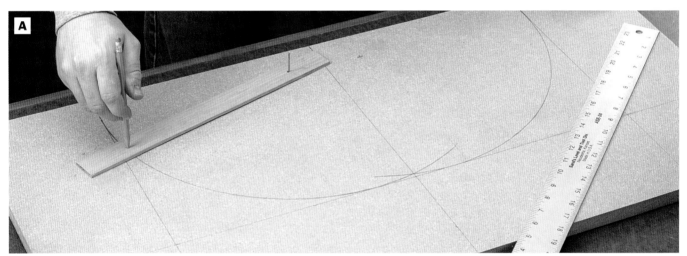

A

Drill ⅛-in. holes 10 in. apart in a thin scrap to create a compass for drawing the arcs on the top of the bending jig.

B

Use a combination square to scribe the inside curve line ¾ in. in from the edge of the inside curve of the jig.

After rough cutting the strips, mill them to the final ⅛-in. thickness with a planer. (See text for how to use a planer that can't be adjusted to ⅛ in.)

Test the laminating jig with a dry run, clamping the strips without any glue. Adjust the sliding end of the clamps in as you force the strips into the jig.

Next, scribe a line ¾ in. in from the curved edge of the inside section of the jig (**Photo B**). Cut just outside this line and sand off the excess. Then reposition the two sections of jig so that there is even spacing along the curve. The spacing between the sections should be slightly more than ¾ in. This space will accommodate the lamination.

Cut the inside section of the jig in half with a miter saw. Then trim the back corners of each half at steep angles to provide a starting notch for the wedges. (The wedges will be used to force the jig against the laminated strips.)

The final step in constructing the jig is to attach the remaining piece of jig material to the bottom of the large curve section of the jig. Position it so that it extends past the front edge of the large curve. This provides both a support area for the strips as you begin clamping and a base to push the strips against and keep them flush.

BENDING THE LAMINATION

Once the jig is complete, you can prepare to laminate. You will need six strips to laminate, but some may break apart in the planer, so make a few extras. Rough cut the strips to about ³⁄₁₆-in. thickness by ripping them with a table saw or resawing them with a band saw. Plane the strips to the final ⅛-in. thickness (**Photo C**).

If your planer will not plane the strips to ⅛ in., build a planer skid to raise the strips closer to the cutterhead. A planer skid is simply a board or piece of plywood that the workpiece rides on through the planer. It should be slightly larger than the strips with a low lip attached to the back edge to keep the strips from being pushed off.

Once the strips are milled, it is time to do a dry run. This is your rehearsal, a critical step in a project that involves large glued surfaces. If a problem is not discovered until the gluing stage, it's easier to start over than to try to salvage the workpieces.

Center the strips and inside jig halves on the outside jig. Begin tightening each clamp a little at a time **(Photo D).** Carefully reset the clamps as they bottom out. When you have fully seated the inside jig halves in the outside jig section, drive wedges between the halves to force pressure on the ends of the lamination.

Look for gaps in the lamination. If there is a gap, disassemble the jig and sand down small areas of the jig adjacent to the gap. Repeat the dry run process until the lamination is tight and free of gaps.

Now you are ready to glue the lamination. I used polyurethane glue for three reasons. First, it has a long open time, allowing me to assemble the jig without rushing. Second, it has a high viscosity, which allows for a very controlled application. Third, after it

is cured, polyurethane glue doesn't allow the pieces to "creep" or shift like PVA (yellow) glue.

Center the first strip on the jig without glue. Then apply glue to only the top face of each strip. Spread the glue with a flat scrap, similar to using a squeegee. Place each glued face against the previous strip in the jig.

Pay close attention to the faces you apply glue to — it is easy to get carried away and apply glue to too many faces. When all the strips are in position, clamp the jig together as you did during the dry run **(Photo E).**

Remove the top rack after the glue has fully cured, at least 24 hours. The rack will lose a small amount of its curve; this is known as spring back. Spring back is affected by several factors including wood species, wood dryness, lamination strip thickness, glue type

Drive wedges between the inside jig halves to apply pressure to the ends of the laminations. Wax paper taped to the jig prevents the lamination from adhering to the jig.

Clean up the dried glue with a chisel or rasp. Then finish the edges of the lamination with a jointer, or use a scraper, hand plane or sander.

Cut ⅜-in.-deep by 2-in.-wide dadoes in the outside faces of the sides. Use a backer board attached to a miter gauge to prevent chipping.

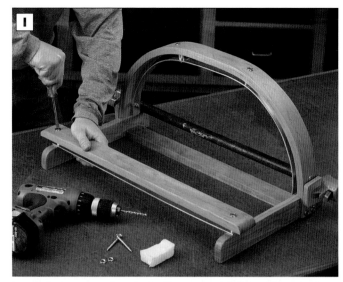

Attach the bottom rack and rail with screws. Drill ⅛-in. pilot holes in the side pieces, and apply beeswax to the screw threads to make them easier to drive.

Attach the bent aluminum rail to the inside of the top rack using machine screws. Cut ¾-in. lengths of ½-in. aluminum tubing as spacers.

and bending radius. I took the specific spring back of this lamination into account when designing the cook's rack. If you decide to create your own projects using bent lamination, do a test lamination to check the amount of spring back.

Cut off the ragged ends of the top rack to the point where a full thickness of the lamination begins. Remove dried glue buildup with a chisel or rasp, and finish the edge with a jointer, scraper or sander **(Photo F).** Cut the end of the rack so that when it is standing upright it is symmetrical and 12 in. tall.

Cut the bottom rack, sides and wall brace to size. Cut a ¾-in. radius in the ends of the bottom rack with a router, or round over with a sander. Use a jigsaw to cut 1-in. radii in the top and bottom corners of the sides. Cut dadoes in the outside faces of each side **(Photo G).** Sand and finish all parts with three coats of wipe-on polyurethane.

ASSEMBLY

I bought the aluminum rail and tubing for the rack at a home center. The rail was malleable enough that I could bend it by hand. I left it long initially and

bent it in small amounts, checking it frequently against the top rack until they matched. I then marked and cut the rail 2 in. shorter on each end than the top rack. The bottom rail is a straight 24-in.-long piece of the same aluminum stock.

Drill four ⁷⁄₃₂-in.-dia. holes located 1 in. up and 3-½-in. and 12-in. in from each end. Transfer these hole locations to the aluminum rail, and drill matching holes at each location. Fasten the rail to the top rack **(Photo H).**

Position the top rack in each side dado, and clamp the wall brace between the sides and top rack. Drill ⅛-in.-dia. pilot holes, and fasten each end with two No. 10 × 2½-in. flathead slotted wood screws with decorative washers to match the fasteners on the top rack and rail.

Then attach the bottom rack to the sides. Drill ⅛-in. pilot holes 2 in. from the bottom of each side and a ⁷⁄₃₂-in. pilot hole through the bottom rail. Attach with the same screws and washers used to fasten the top rack and sides **(Photo I).**

Hang the rack by driving screws through the wall brace into at least one, but preferably two, wall studs. If only one stud falls behind the rack, use a wall toggle as a second fastener to keep the rack level.

Dan Cary, *writer*
Mark Macemon, *photography*
Gabriel Graphics, *illustration*

Versatile Valet

Some woodworking projects require tricky joinery techniques or demand that you tame beautiful but highly uncooperative wood. This is not one of them. The biggest challenge in building this project will come when you try to describe exactly what you've made. Is it a cabinet? A table? A display stand? All we know for sure is that it is useful, versatile, easy to build and pleasing to look at. You're not likely to find the term in any furniture catalog, but we've dubbed this household furnishing a "valet cabinet." Based loosely on a conglomeration of familiar styles, it is straightforward enough in appearance to fit into just about any home.

Versatile Valet

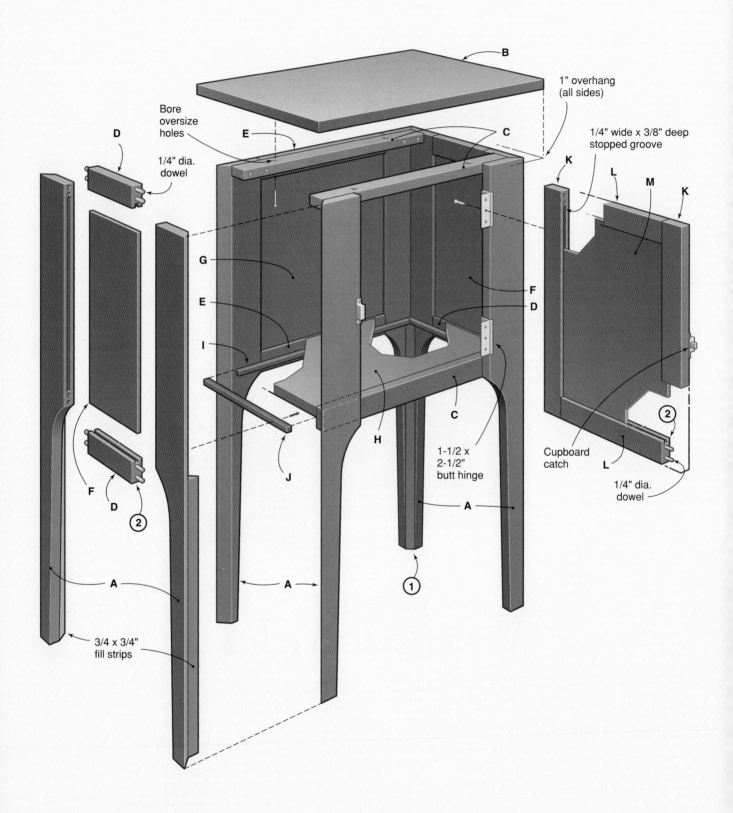

B

1" overhang
(all sides)

Bore
oversize
holes

D

1/4" dia.
dowel

E

C

1/4" wide x 3/8" deep
stopped groove

K

L

M

K

G

F

E

D

I

F

J

H

C

1-1/2 x
2-1/2"
butt hinge

A

Cupboard
catch

L

1/4" dia.
dowel

②

F

D

②

A

A

①

3/4 x 3/4"
fill strips

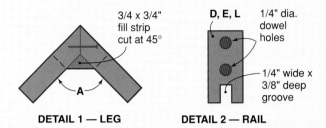

3/4 x 3/4"
fill strip
cut at 45°

A

DETAIL 1 — LEG

D, E, L

1/4" dia.
dowel
holes

1/4" wide x
3/8" deep
groove

DETAIL 2 — RAIL

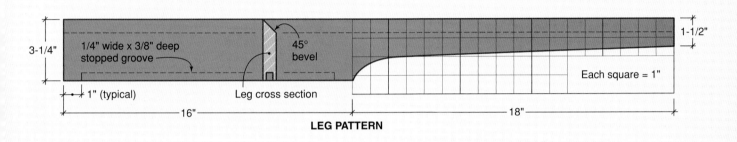

3-1/4"

1/4" wide x 3/8" deep
stopped groove

45°
bevel

Leg cross section

1" (typical)

16"

1-1/2"

Each square = 1"

18"

LEG PATTERN

Shopping List

- ☐ 1½ × 2½-in. butt hinges (2)
- ☐ Cupboard catch (Rockler No. 32860)
- ☐ ¼-in. wood dowels
- ☐ No. 8 × 1¼-in. panhead screws (4)
- ☐ No. 8 wood screws (1¼ and 2 in.)
- ☐ 1-in. brads
- ☐ Wood glue

Materials and Cutting List

Part/Description		No.	Size
A	Legs	8	¾ × 3¼ × 34 in.
B	Top	1	¾ × 14 × 20 in.
C	Stretchers	3	¾ × 1½ × 16½ in.
D	Side rails	4	¾ × 1½ × 5½ in.
E	Back rails	2	¾ × 1½ × 11½ in.
F	Side panels	2	¼ × 6 × 13½ in.
G	Back panel	1	¼ × 12 × 13½ in.
H	Bottom	1	¾ × 9¾ × 16½ in.
I	Cleats	2	⅜ × ⅜ × 15½ in.
J	Cleats	2	⅜ × ⅜ × 11 in.
K	Door stiles	2	¾ × 1½ × 15¾ in.
L	Door rails	2	¾ × 1½ × 11¼ in.
M	Door panel	1	¾ × 11¾ × 13½ in.

In the bathroom, the valet cabinet can function as a washstand or a small supplementary vanity that holds hand towels or grooming products. It's also a good fit in a dining room for displaying a silverware chest and storing table linens. You can position it near a door as a resting spot for gloves and keys or put it in the kitchen to use as a spare work surface or a microwave stand. You can even add a lock to the door and convert it to a minibar.

ABOUT THE DESIGN

If you described the style of this cabinet as Shaker, you wouldn't be too far off the mark. The wood species, the finish, the wide rails and stiles, the inset frame-and-panel doors, the curve of the tapered legs, the overhanging top and the overall tone of the piece all borrow from Shaker design. The cabinet shown stands just under 35 in. tall, so it is closer to counter-top height than table height. This is convenient for use in a kitchen or bathroom. For other rooms, you may want to consider shortening the legs from 34 in. to about 29 in. But be aware that changing the height will detract from the cabinet's appearance.

The joints in the door frame and in the side and back panel assemblies are reinforced with ¼-in.-dia. dowels. Dowel joints can be tricky to align, but they're easier to make than many other joints. I used inexpensive metal dowel points as guides for drilling the dowel holes.

The tabletop is made from two pieces of edge-glued stock. To allow for wood movement on this wide part, I attached it to the base with screws driven through oversize guide holes in the stretchers.

Relatively small furnishings such as this cabinet often are made with wood that is not heavily figured. Maple, birch, poplar, beech and red alder are suitable hardwoods, but you can use a figured wood if you prefer. I chose red alder because it is workable and relatively inexpensive.

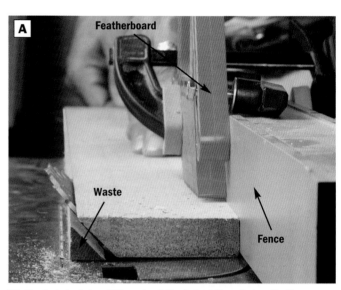

Rip the leg stock to width and cut the leg sections to length; then bevel-rip a 45-degree miter on one edge of each leg section. The table saw blade should tilt away from the fence.

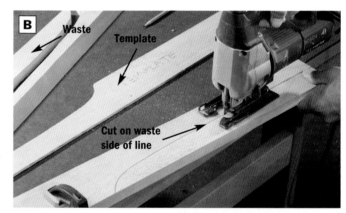

Make a template for the leg section profile, using the pattern in the drawing as a guide. Trace the profile onto each of the leg sections and then rough cut them with a jigsaw. Make the cuts slightly on the waste side of the cutting lines.

The most efficient way to build this project is to make the side assemblies and the back and front assemblies and then join them into a case by creating the long bevel-miter joints at each leg corner. Next, make and install the door, fasten the bottom panel on wood cleats and glue up and attach the top panel.

MAKE THE PARTS

Mill all of the stock to uniform thickness (¾ in.) and then rip material for the legs (3¼ in.) and the rails and stiles (1½ in.). Also rip and cross-cut stock for the edge-glued top panel (14 × 20 in.). Glue up the

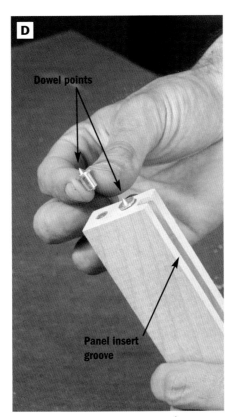

Dowel points

Panel insert groove

Panel insert groove

Refine the profiles using an oscillating spindle sander (above) or a router with a template-following bit. Clamp all eight sections together and even them out with a belt sander if the profiles vary (inset photo).

To make the dowel joints, drill two ¼-in. holes in each end of each rail, making sure to keep the drill parallel with the side of the workpiece. Insert a ¼-in. dowel point into each hole.

Using a framing square as a reference, press the rail with the dowel points against the mating board. The points in the end of the rail will make impressions in the mating board.

top panel using biscuits or dowels to aid alignment.

Next, cut the legs, rails and stiles to length. Mount a ¼-in. straight bit in a router table and cut centered, ⅜-in.-deep grooves in the edges of six of the eight leg parts. Start the 14-in.-long grooves in the legs 1 in. from the top ends.

Make the 45-degree bevel-rip cut on the inside edge of each leg part with a table saw (Photo A). Feed the parts into the blade with the waste side of the cut farther from the fence. (With the saw I used, that meant moving the fence to the left side of the blade.) Save the 45-degree-beveled cutoff pieces to use as fill strips/corner blocks on each leg.

Make a template of the leg profile using the drawing on p. 55 as a guide. Trace the template profile onto each leg and then cut out the profile with a jigsaw, favoring the waste side of the cutting line (Photo B). I refined each leg profile individually with an oscillating spindle sander (Photo C) and then ganged all eight boards together and sanded them to a uniform profile with a belt sander. If you're handy with a router, you could use a pattern and a flush-trim bit instead of sanding.

Cut the insert panels and the bottom panel to size.

Although you can find alder plywood, it typically comes in ¾-in.-thick 4×8 sheets that cost at least $75. Instead, I bought a 2×4 panel of ¼-in. birch plywood (which also seemed overpriced at $17). The color is slightly paler than the red alder, but the grain patterns are similar, and after being stained the panels matched pretty well.

ASSEMBLE THE CABINET

Drill two ¼ × ¾-in. dowel holes in the end of each rail (including the door rails), keeping the holes away from the panel insert grooves. Use a drill press or right-angle drilling guide where possible to ensure that the holes are straight.

Insert a ¼-in. dowel point (Photo D) into each dowel hole and press the mating stile or leg against each rail to mark drilling points (Photo E). Drill at the points, again taking care to keep the drill bit straight and perpendicular to the workpiece. Insert ¼-dia. wood dowels into the dowel holes and test the fit of each joint (Photo F). Glue and clamp the four assemblies. (Work carefully — the thin, beveled edges are very delicate.) Don't forget to insert the correct panel into the grooves in the sides, back and door

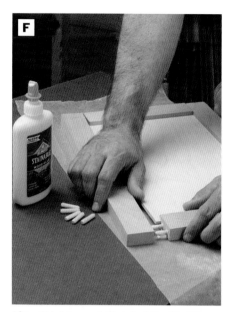

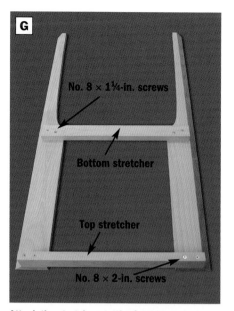

No. 8 × 1¼-in. screws

Bottom stretcher

Top stretcher

No. 8 × 2-in. screws

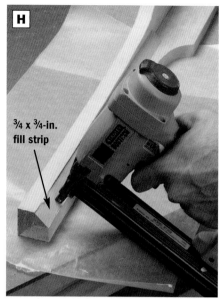

¾ x ¾-in. fill strip

After all joints are drilled, test the fit of the parts and then clamp and glue the project up into sections. Do not glue the panels that are inset into the door, sides and back.

Attach the stretchers to the front leg sections using countersunk wood screws. The top stretcher is installed on edge with No. 8 × 2-in. wood screws, and the bottom stretcher is installed on the flat with No. 8 × 1¼-in. screws.

Glue the assemblies together, fastening each bevel-miter joint in a few spots with brads. Glue and pin-nail the 45-degree fill strips at the inside corner of each leg.

before glue-up, and be sure to keep glue off of the panel edges.

Before gluing the assemblies together to form the case, attach the stretchers between the front legs and at the top of the back assembly (**Photo G**). Fasten the stretchers with countersunk No. 8 wood screws (2 in. long for the upper stretchers and 1¼ in. long for the lower front stretcher). Glue the legs together one pair at a time to create each corner. Because the length of these bevel-miter joints increases the chances of ending up with small gaps at the seams, I used a stainable wood glue from Elmer's. Pin-nail each joint in several locations with 1-in. (18-gauge) brads.

To make more substantial legs, cut long corner blocks from the ¾ × ¾-in. triangular cutoffs that you trimmed from each leg during bevel-ripping. Glue the corner blocks into the crotch of each corner (**Photo H**) and then (**Photo I**) file or sand edges where necessary.

Nail and glue the cleats so that the top edges are ¾ in. below the tops of the bottom stretcher and lower rails, and then attach the bottom panel of the cabinet to the cleats with screws or brads. Center the door in the opening and hang it with butt hinges. Drill extra-large guide holes in the stretchers; then center the top panel on the cabinet base. Attach the top with panhead screws driven up through the stretcher guide holes. The extra space in the guide holes allows the wood to move slightly as changes in humidity cause expansion and contraction.

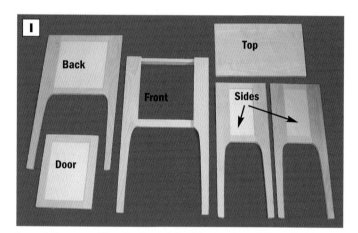

Back

Top

Front

Sides

Door

Lay out the assemblies for the valet cabinet and sand them, finishing with 150-grit sandpaper. Do not sand the long beveled edges. The bottom panel (made of melamine-coated particleboard that does not require sanding) and cleats are not shown.

Finally, apply your choice of finish. I used a dark maple stain (General Finishes Maple Wood Stain) to even out the red alder and birch plywood tones and then applied a few coats of wipe-on varnish to preserve and protect the finish.

Mark Johanson, *writer, photography*
Scott Jacobson, *photography*
Gabriel Graphics, *illustration*

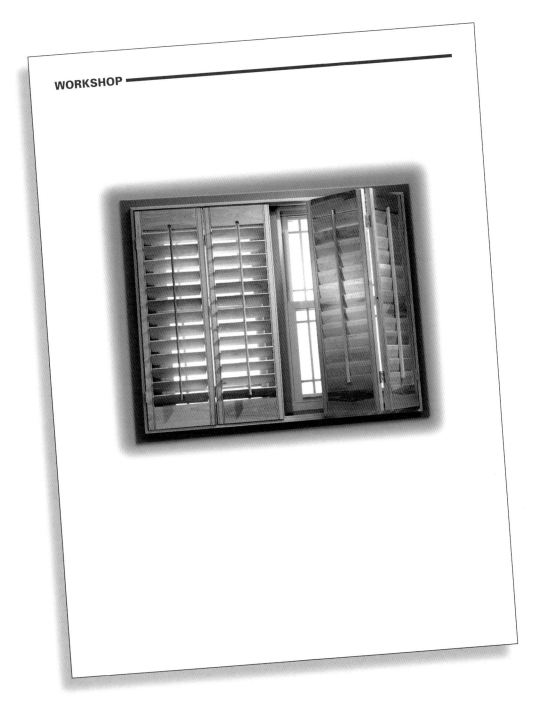

Plantation Shutters

Plantation shutters have long been admired for their beauty and mechanical elegance. Although the name reflects their association with the South, these high-end window treatments have been used around the world for hundreds of years. Their characteristic wide louvers — at least 2 in. — provide maximum light protection and airflow control. But this level of quality comes at a steep price, often as much as $300 to cover one double-hung window.

Plantation Shutters

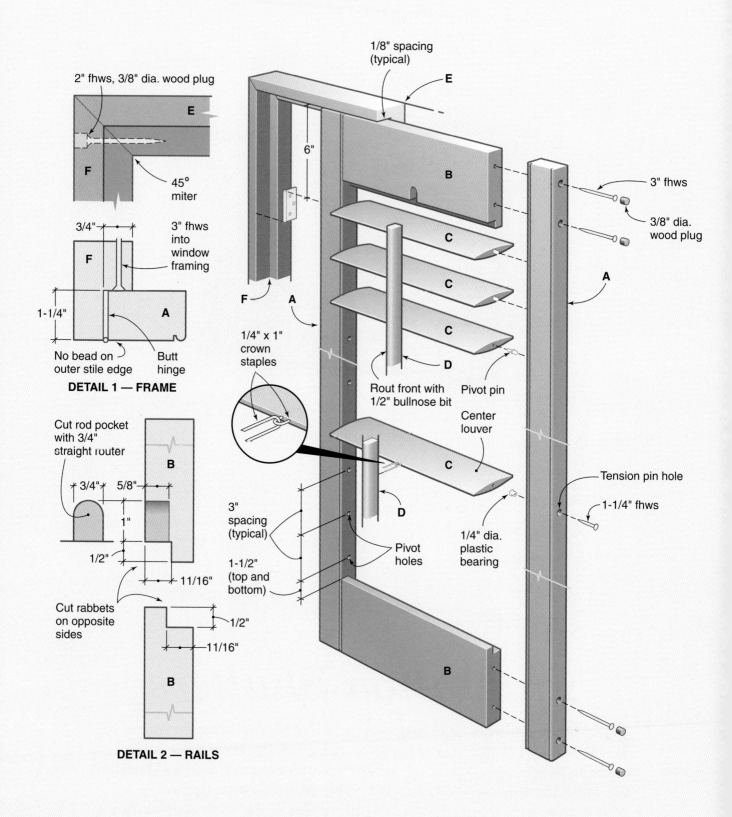

2" fhws, 3/8" dia. wood plug

E

F

45° miter

3/4"

F

3" fhws into window framing

1-1/4"

A

No bead on outer stile edge

Butt hinge

DETAIL 1 — FRAME

Cut rod pocket with 3/4" straight router

B

3/4" 5/8"

1"

1/2"

11/16"

Cut rabbets on opposite sides

1/2"

11/16"

B

DETAIL 2 — RAILS

1/8" spacing (typical)

E

6"

B

C

C

C

D

Rout front with 1/2" bullnose bit

Pivot pin

Center louver

1/4" x 1" crown staples

3" spacing (typical)

1-1/2" (top and bottom)

Pivot holes

D

C

1/4" dia. plastic bearing

B

F   A

A

3" fhws

3/8" dia. wood plug

A

Tension pin hole

1-1/4" fhws

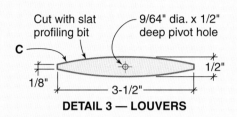

Cut with slat profiling bit

9/64" dia. x 1/2" deep pivot hole

C

1/8"

1/2"

3-1/2"

DETAIL 3 — LOUVERS

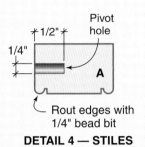

1/2"

Pivot hole

1/4"

A

Rout edges with 1/4" bead bit

DETAIL 4 — STILES

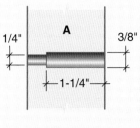

1/4"

A

3/8"

1-1/4"

**DETAIL 5
TENSION PIN HOLE**

Shopping List

- [ ] 65 lineal ft. 1 × 4
- [ ] 45 lineal ft. 2 × 4
- [ ] 10 lineal ft. 2 × 4
- [ ] $\frac{3}{8}$-in. hole plugs
- [ ] $\frac{1}{4}$-in. × 1-in. crown staples
- [ ] 2-in. screws
- [ ] 3-in. screws
- [ ] (8) $1\frac{3}{4}$ × $2\frac{1}{2}$-in. butt hinges (Stanley 81-9101)
- [ ] (4) Magnetic door catches
- [ ] Woodline Plantation Shutter Router Bit Set (WL 2055)
- [ ] Woodline Shutter Louver Pin Kit (WL 2055-1)

Makes four panels

Panel Cutting List

Part/Description		No.	Size
A	Stiles	2	$1\frac{1}{4} \times 2 \times 48\frac{3}{4}$ in.
B	Rails	2	$1\frac{1}{4} \times 5 \times 12\frac{3}{16}$ in.
C	Louvers	13	$\frac{1}{2} \times 3\frac{1}{2} \times 12\frac{1}{8}$ in.
D	Control rod	1	$\frac{1}{2} \times 1 \times 38\frac{1}{2}$ in.

Frame Cutting List

E	Frame top/bottom	2	$1\frac{1}{2} \times 2 \times 64\frac{7}{8}$ in.
F	Frame sides	2	$1\frac{1}{2} \times 2 \times 52$ in.

Dimensions are for one set of $50\frac{3}{8}$-in. × $63\frac{3}{8}$-in. bifold shutters.
One panel (build four)
*All wood is furniture grade

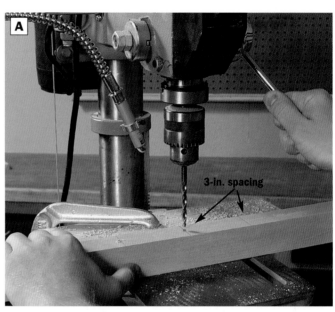

A laser pointer mounted to the drill press is indexed to the hole positions in the stile for the pivot pins.

When we heard about a new router bit set designed to help DIYers build shutters for as little as a quarter of the cost of manufactured ones, we had to give it a try. Wayne Sutter of Woodline USA visited our shop to demonstrate how the system worked, and he built these bifold shutters in one day.

Although the machining techniques involved in building the shutters are not difficult, planning is critical. Because each shutter is designed and built to fit a specific window size, you must take the time to determine exact measurements and dimensions of the parts. And each installation will pose challenges that may require design modifications.

DETERMINE STYLE AND SIZE

Because the wall space on one side of our window was limited, we built bifold shutters. The dimensions in the Cutting List (p. 61) are for building one set of bifold shutters and frames with an overall size of $50\frac{3}{8} \times 63\frac{3}{8}$-in.

Determining the size of the shutters for your situation is the most important step in the process. Start by deciding whether you want the shutters to cover the entire window and casing, to attach to the casing or to fit inside the casing. We mounted our shutters over the existing casing. This way we could leave

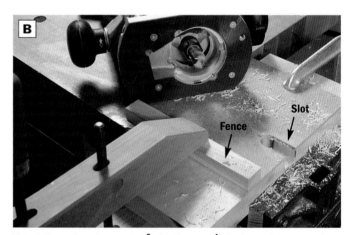

To cut the rod pocket, rout a $\frac{5}{8}$-in.-deep $\times$ $1\frac{1}{2}$-in.-long slot centered in the bottom front face of the top rail.

Woodline's shutter kit includes five router bits and a packet of 50 louver pins and four tension bushings.

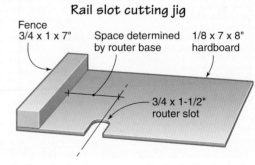

Rail slot cutting jig

Fence
3/4 x 1 x 7"

Space determined by router base

1/8 x 7 x 8" hardboard

3/4 x 1-1/2" router slot

To make the jig, attach a fence perpendicular to the front edge of the $\frac{1}{4}$-in. hardboard. Next, rout a $\frac{3}{4}$-in. $\times$ $1\frac{1}{2}$-in. slot into the hardboard to establish the cut line.

some of the casing exposed to tie in with the rest of the trim in the room.

If you want to leave the full casing exposed, you can remove the existing casing, install the shutters and then replace the casing around the shutters. Or, if the window is set inside the opening at least 2 in., you can mount the shutters inside the window frame.

Another consideration when determining shutter size is the location of the wall framing. Whenever possible, the side frame pieces should be mounted to

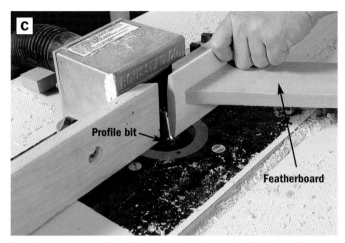

Rout the curved ranch profile on all four edges of each louver. Use a featherboard to hold the stock against the router table's fence.

Center the bit on the end of the louver. Raise each louver up to the drill bit.

existing wall framing to ensure that they'll be securely anchored.

Measure and record the dimensions of the total area the shutter panels and shutter frames will cover. Then use the equations in "Sizing Your Shutters," (p. 65) to determine the dimensions of individual parts.

MAKE THE PANEL PARTS

The panels are identical, so plan to machine and assemble all of the parts for each panel at the same time.

Begin by cutting the rails and stiles to size. Using the ¼-in. bead bit, rout the vertical edges of each stile. Then bore ¼-in.-dia. × ½-in.-deep holes for the louver pins centered along the inside edge of each stile **(Photo A).** Locate the first hole 1½ in. from the inside edge of the rail. The remaining holes must be spaced exactly 3 in. apart to ensure smooth shutter operation.

The louvers are held open by the tension created by a screw driven through the outside edge of the stile and into one of the middle louvers.

The screw runs through a ¼-in.-dia. plastic bearing called a tension bearing, which is seated in the stile.

Create the tension screw hole by drilling through one of the middle pin holes already in the stile with a

Louver pin drilling jig

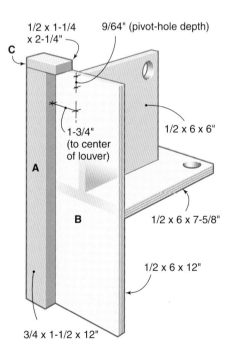

Side fence (A), back face (B) and stop block (C) are attached to a simple T-base that clamps to any drill press table.

Hold the jig flush with the side of the louver and drive a 1-in.-long crown staple into one edge of each louver.

Louver stapling jig

1/8"-deep recess
(5/8 x 3/4" or
to fit stapler)

1/4 x 1/2 x 3-1/2"

A

3/4 x 2 x 11"

1/4"-dia.
hole

1"

6-1/16"

1/2"-deep slot to fit louver edge

Position the top hole of the jig over the center of the louver's edge. The jig should be registered against one louver end. Position the fence (A) so the stapler shoots squarely into the louver's edge.

¼-in. bit. Then, drilling from the outside edge of the stile, enlarge the ¼-in. hole to ⅜-in. dia. × 1½ in. deep. This creates a countersink for the head of the tension screw (see drawing, p. 61, detail 5).

Next, cut the rails to size. When the louvers are closed, the control rod fits into a clearance slot in the top rail. Rout the slot using the ¾-in. straight bit and a simple straightedge jig (**Photo B and drawing**). Complete the rails, using the ⅜-in. router bit to cut a ⅜-in.-wide × ¹¹⁄₁₆-in.-deep rabbet along the bottom front edge of the top rail and along the top back edge of the bottom rail.

The louvers are sized to fit between the stiles,

All staples should protrude out of the louver about ¼ in. Tap down high staples with a tack hammer.

leaving ¹⁄₃₂-in. clearance on each side. Plane the louver stock to ½ in. thick and cut it to size. The louvers are tapered so they're thicker in the center and thinner along the edges. Create the taper using the slat-profiling bit with the router table (**Photo C**). If you're using hardwood, make these cuts in two or three passes to limit chipping and chatter.

Next, drill ⁹⁄₆₄-in.-dia. × ½-in.-deep louver pin holes in the ends of each louver (**Photo D and drawing**).

The final part to make for each panel is the control rod. Cut the control rod to size, and use the ½-in. bullnose bit to round over the front face edges.

ASSEMBLE THE LOUVERS

Each louver is connected to the control rod with a pair of 1-in.-long crown staples. The staples interlock, with one staple in the edge of the louver and the other staple in the control rod. To accomplish this tricky connection, build two stapling jigs to accommodate your crown stapler. The jigs we built work with a Senco FinishPro 2N1.

The louver stapling jig (**Photo E and drawing**) is designed to position the staple along the edge of the louver and leave approximately ¼ in. of the staple exposed. Test the jig on some scrap louver stock to adjust staple placement and depth. After driving a staple into each louver, line up the louvers and make sure all of the staples are at the same height (**Photo F**).

The control rod stapling jig (**Photo G and drawing**) is designed to position the control rod and louvers so that the second staple is centered on the control rod edge and overlaps the existing louver staple. Again, it's best to test the positioning on scrap pieces first. Drive staples into the control rod at 3-in. intervals beginning 1 in. from one end of the control rod.

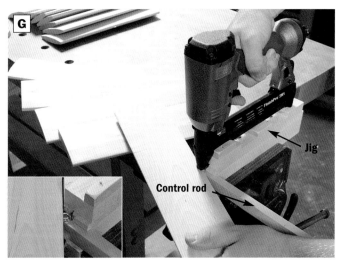

Secure the control rod to the jig with a spring clamp. Place each louver at an angle against the jig and over the control rod. Drive a staple into the control rod so that it couples with the existing louver staple (see inset).

Control rod stapling jig

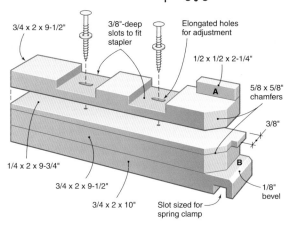

3/4 x 2 x 9-1/2"
3/8"-deep slots to fit stapler
Elongated holes for adjustment
1/2 x 1/2 x 2-1/4"
A
5/8 x 5/8" chamfers
3/8"
1/4 x 2 x 9-3/4"
B
3/4 x 2 x 9-1/2"
1/8" bevel
3/4 x 2 x 10"
Slot sized for spring clamp

The staple gun's magazine registers against stop block (A) and the control rod rests on the base (B).

Slip the louver pins into the first stile, working from one end to the other. Lift up the louvers slightly with the control rod to help align them.

Sizing your shutters

The following equations will provide the dimensions necessary for building bifold shutters with 3½-in. louvers.

1. Determine the overall height and width to be covered by the shutters:
   When installing shutters with a mounting frame, measure the height and width of the entire area to be covered and subtract 1½ in. from each. (This accounts for the extra width added by the frame.) For shutters without the mounting frame (inside mount), measure the inside window frame height and width.

2. Determine the panel dimensions:
   Panel height = Total shutter opening height − ¼ in.
   Panel width = (Total shutter width ÷ number of shutters) − ³⁄₁₆ in.

3. Determine the number of louvers: (Panel height in inches − 10) ÷ 3. Round up to the nearest whole number.

4. Determine the panel part dimensions:
   Stiles:
   Thickness = 1¼ in.
   Width = 2 in.
   Length = Panel height
   Rails:
   Thickness = 1¼ in.
   Width = Panel height − (Number of louvers × 3) ÷ 2
   Length = Panel width − 4 in.
   Louvers:
   Thickness = ½ in.
   Width = 3½ in.
   Length = Rail length − ¹⁄₁₆ in.
   Control rod:
   Thickness = ½ in.
   Width = 1 in.
   Approximate length = Stile length − (Rail width × 2) − ¼ in.
   Mounting frame:
   Thickness = 2½ in.
   Width = 1¼ in.
   Length = Total opening dimensions

After aligning all louver pins, drive two screws through each stile and into the rails. Be sure the panel is square before securing.

Drive a 1¼-in. screw through the tension screw hole (see drawing) and into the tension bushing and louver.

Mount the frame with 3-in. screws driven through the frame and into the wall framing.

ASSEMBLE THE PANELS

Secure the rails to one of the stiles with two countersunk 2½-in. screws. Insert a louver pin in each louver hole except for the one that lines up with the tension pin hole in the stile. Fit the louver pins into the stile that is attached to the rails (**Photo H, p. 65).** After installing one side of the louvers, position the second stile and repeat the process. When you have inserted all of the louver pins, clamp the stiles and rails together and secure them with countersunk 2½-in. screws (**photo I).** Plug the countersink holes with ⅜-in. plugs. Then install the tension screw and tighten it to the desired resistance (**Photo J).**

If you are building single-panel shutters, at this point you are ready to build the frame and install the shutters. But for bifold shutters, you must first connect each pair of shutters with two butt hinges. Position the hinges 6 in. from the top and bottom edges of the shutters.

BUILD THE FRAME

The shutters hang on a frame that is mounted directly to the wall (or through the window casing and into the wall). The frame is similar to the back side of a picture frame. It features mitered corners and a ¾-in.-wide × 1¼-in.-deep rabbet cut around the inside edge. The shutters hang on hinges and fit into the rabbet opening.

Unless you are making large shutters, it is easiest to build the frames on a flat surface and then attach them to the wall. This helps ensure proper shutter operation.

Position the frame pieces on a flat surface. Attach hinges to the outside edges of the shutters and position them inside the frame. Insert strips of ⅛-in. hardboard to maintain the gaps between and around the shutters. Check that the frame is square, and countersink 2-in. screws through the miters.

Before removing the shutters or moving the frame, mark the hinge positions. Carefully remove the shutters, and tack scraps diagonally across the frame to keep it square. Position the frame over the window, and drive 3-in. screws through the frame rabbets (**Photo K).** Hang the shutters by attaching the hinges to the frame.

If the shutters rub or are too tight, remove them and trim an equal amount from both shutters. Finally, install magnetic catches to keep the shutters closed.

Dan Cary, *writer*

Larry Okrend and Mark Macemon, *photography*

Wayne Sutter, *project design*

Simonton Windows, *windows*

Gabriel Graphics, *illustration*

Finer Futon Frame

Although still relative newcomers in the American home furnishings market, convertible futon sofas are starting to mature. The original inexpensive wood-pallet or tube-steel versions continue to hold a strong position on the lower end of the futon-frame spectrum, but innovative furniture makers and futon specialty shops have improved both the quality and styling of higher-end models. The futon frame shown here jumps on the finer-futon bandwagon, combining simple efficiency with solid construction techniques and slightly more sophisticated styling.

Finer Futon Frame

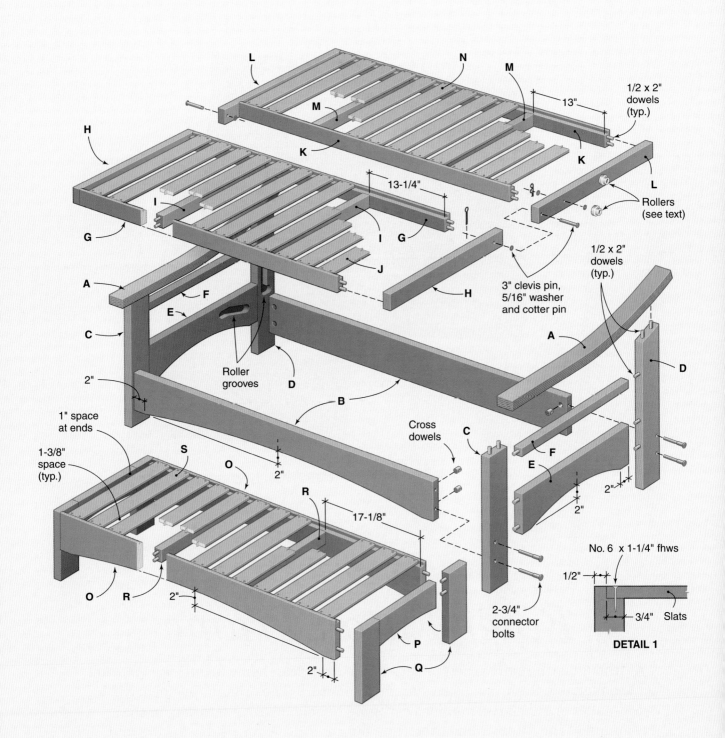

L

N

M

1/2 x 2" dowels (typ.)

13"

M

H

K

K

L

M

13-1/4"

I

I

G

Rollers (see text)

G

I

1/2 x 2" dowels (typ.)

J

A

F

H

E

A

C

D

Roller grooves

D

B

2"

C

1" space at ends

Cross dowels

F

E

1-3/8" space (typ.)

S

O

D

2"

2"

R

17-1/8"

2"

O

R

2"

P

2-3/4" connector bolts

Q

No. 6 x 1-1/4" fhws

1/2"

3/4"   Slats

DETAIL 1

3" clevis pin, 5/16" washer and cotter pin

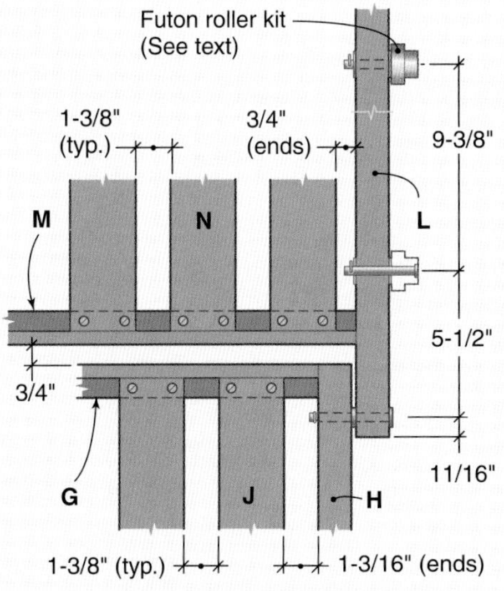

Futon roller kit
(See text)
1-3/8"
(typ.)
3/4"
(ends)
9-3/8"
M
N
L
5-1/2"
3/4"
11/16"
G
J
H
1-3/8" (typ.)
1-3/16" (ends)

BACKREST AND SEAT DETAILS

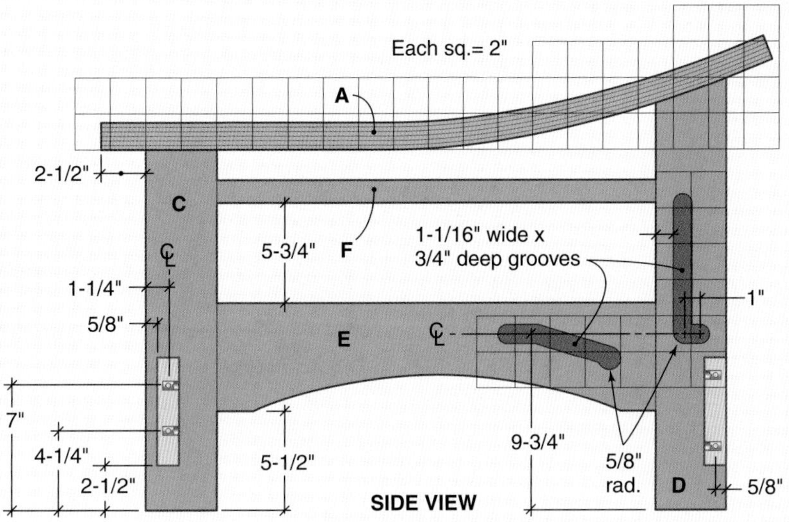

Each sq.= 2"
A
2-1/2"
C
F
5-3/4"
1-1/16" wide x
3/4" deep grooves
1-1/4"
1"
5/8"
E
7"
4-1/4"
2-1/2"
5-1/2"
9-3/4"
5/8"
rad.
D
5/8"

SIDE VIEW

Shopping List

- ☐ 100 bf 6/4 ash (6+ in. wide)
- ☐ 4 futon rollers with hardware (or 1-in.-dia. maple doweling)
- ☐ ½ × 2-in. wood dowels
- ☐ 1¼-in. flathead wood screws
- ☐ (8) ¼ × 2¾-in. connector bolts with 7/16-in.-dia. cross dowels
- ☐ (2) ¼ × 3-in. clevis pins with cotter pins and 5/16-in. washers
- ☐ 21 × 54-in. futon mattress with cover; 52 to 54 × 54-in. futon mattress with cover
- ☐ Polyurethane glue, PVA glue
- ☐ Finishing materials

Materials and Cutting List

Part/Description	No.	Size
A Arms (laminated)	2	1½ × 2½ × 38 in.
B Sofa rails	2	1¼ × 6 × 54 in.
C Front legs	2	1¼ × 4 × 20 in.
D Back legs	2	1¼ × 4 × 24 in.
E Side rails	2	1¼ × 6 × 24½ in.
F Side spreaders	2	1¼ × 1¼ × 24½ in.
G Seat frame front/back	2	1¼ × 2½ × 47¾ in.
H Seat frame sides	2	1¼ × 2½ × 26 in.
I Seat spreaders	2	1¼ × 2 × 23½ in.
J Seat slats	12	½ × 2½ × 25 in.
K Back frame front/back	2	1¼ × 2½ × 50½ in.
L Back frame sides	2	1¼ × 2½ × 28¾ in.
M Back frame spreaders	2	1¼ × 2 × 22¾ in.
N Back frame slats	13	½ × 2½ × 24¼ in.
O Ottoman rails	2	1¼ × 6 × 51 in.
P Ottoman sides	2	1¼ × 6 × 13 in.
Q Ottoman legs	4	1¼ × 4 × 11 in.
R Ottoman spreaders	2	1¼ × 2 × 18½ in.
S Ottoman slats	13	1¼ × 2½ × 20 in.

The footprint of the plan is a loveseat-style sofa with an accompanying ottoman. Together they provide compact, comfortable seating that occupies less than 60 in. of wall space — compared with about 80 in. for a standard full-size bifold futon. But when butted together, the flattened sofa frame and the ottoman convert into a spacious, full-size bed.

The separate mattresses for the sofa and ottoman do not detract from sleeping comfort. And if you prefer, the ottoman frame can be topped with a piece of beveled glass to create a low coffee table. (The ottoman mattress tucks neatly behind the sofa frame.) Either way, this futon and ottoman set is appropriate for any decor, regardless of whether it's casual or formal.

Because it is strong, springy and inexpensive, we used white ash to construct the furniture frames and slats. The mattresses (54 × 54 in. and 21 × 54 in.) and mattress covers can be ordered from any futon

supplier and may even be in stock at larger futon stores. The only specialty hardware items needed are the nylon rollers that are attached to the backrest frame and move in routed grooves to create the conversion mechanism.

LAMINATED ARMS

The gentle slope of the sofa arms adds a sense of flow to the overall design and takes advantage of the outstanding bending properties of ash. You can use several methods to bend wood. I opted to cut thin strips of ash and laminate them together in a bending form made from face-glued plywood. This method has excellent strength and results in a top laminate strip with contiguous grain. When form-bending with laminate strips, use polyurethane glue because it resists "creeping" and has a long open time.

To make the plywood bending form, cut three strips of ¾-in. plywood to roughly 10 × 48 in. Face-glue and screw them together, making sure the edges are flush. Then plot out the curve for the arm (see drawing, p. 69) on one face of the workpiece. Follow the cutting line with a band saw or jigsaw; then sand the cuts slightly so they're smooth.

To make the 1½-in.-thick arms, resaw (Photo A) and plane your stock into twelve ¼ × 3 × 48-in. strips (six strips per arm). Plane or sand the strips so the

Resaw the laminated arm strips slightly wider than their 2½-in. finished width. Use a band saw with a pivot jig, or rip them on a table saw.

Make a plywood bending jig; then clamp the plies between the halves of the jig to make the bent arms.

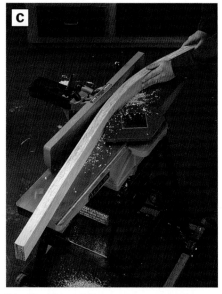

Trim the edges of the arms on your jointer. Joint them until both edges are flat and the arm width is 2½ in.

To make the side assemblies for the sofa frame and ottoman frame, join the side rails and spreaders to the front and back legs. Use a doweling jig and ½-in.-dia. × 2-in. dowels.

Trace the profile of the bent arms onto the top edge of each back leg to create trim lines for the legs. Trim with a jigsaw.

Use one half of the bending form as a drill backer to ensure that the dowel holes in the arms are vertical.

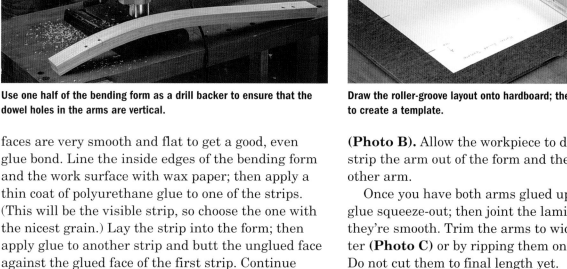

Draw the roller-groove layout onto hardboard; then cut out the grooves to create a template.

faces are very smooth and flat to get a good, even glue bond. Line the inside edges of the bending form and the work surface with wax paper; then apply a thin coat of polyurethane glue to one of the strips. (This will be the visible strip, so choose the one with the nicest grain.) Lay the strip into the form; then apply glue to another strip and butt the unglued face against the glued face of the first strip. Continue adding strips until you have six of them in the form. Clamp the strips together on one end. Then begin clamping the two halves of the form together, sandwiching the strips between them. Use plenty of clamps, tightening each clamp until both faces of the glued block conform with the edges of the form

(**Photo B**). Allow the workpiece to dry overnight, strip the arm out of the form and then glue up the other arm.

Once you have both arms glued up, chisel off the glue squeeze-out; then joint the laminated edges until they're smooth. Trim the arms to width on your jointer (**Photo C**) or by ripping them on your table saw. Do not cut them to final length yet.

SOFA SIDES

The sofa sides are joined with dowels and glue. Plane, joint and cut the front legs, back legs, side rails and side spreaders to size. The back legs should be left square on top at this point. Use a

Use a straight bit with a template collar to rout the roller grooves into the sofa-frame sides.

Lay out the arcs on the bottoms of the frame rails by bending a strip of hardboard into a smooth arc and tracing it on each workpiece.

doweling jig as a guide for drilling the dowel holes in the parts **(Photo D).**

Lay one of the arms across the top of one side assembly so the arm overhangs the front leg by at least 2½ in. The flat portion of the arm should be parallel to the rails and spreaders. Adjust the arm so the slope begins about 8 in. from the inside edge of the back leg. Mark trim lines on the arm, square to the top surface of the arm, 2½ in. past the front leg and 3 in. past the back leg. Transfer the trim lines to the other arm; then square-cut both to length with a handsaw or power miter saw. Use the arms to mark cutting lines on the tops of the back legs **(Photo E);** then trim the tops of both back legs to match the arm profile. Label the arms and sides so you can keep track of which arm was traced onto which side.

To mount the arms to the side assemblies, first drill a pair of dowel holes in the top edge of each leg. Insert dowel points into the holes, position the arms over the dowel points and press down firmly to mark centerpoints in the undersides of the arms. Bore these dowel holes with a drill press, using the bending form as a drill backer to help you orient each arm so the dowel holes will be exactly vertical **(Photo F).** Do not glue the arms on yet.

For its conversion mechanism, this futon frame uses 1-in.-dia. nylon rollers mounted to the backrest and fitted into grooves in the inside faces of the side assemblies. If you use futon roller hardware, make sure to read the instructions that come with it carefully — the required sizes, shapes and locations of the grooves may vary among manufacturers. The instruc-

Join the sofa legs to the front and back rails with connector bolts that fit into cross dowels inserted into holes in the rails.

tions also may require that you alter the width of the backrest frame to create gaps of a different size between the backrest and the side assemblies (as shown, there is a ½-in.-wide gap between each end of the backrest frame and the sofa side). An alternative to futon rollers is to attach fixed 1-in.-dia. maple dowels to the frame to slide (not roll) in the grooves.

Make a hardboard template to use as a guide for routing the grooves in the side assemblies. Draw the groove layout onto the template board; then carefully cut out the grooves in the hardboard with a jigsaw **(Photo G).** Smooth the edges of the grooves; then position the template over each side assembly in turn. Cut the grooves in at least three passes with a router and straight bit fitted with a template collar **(Photo H).** It's always a good idea to make some practice cuts first on scrap wood.

FRONT/BACK SOFA RAILS

Plane, joint and cut the front and back rails to size. The back rail should remain square, but the front rail is cut with a smooth arc on the bottom edge. To lay out the arc, bend a strip of hardboard from the arc ends to the apex; then trace the arc formed by the hardboard onto the rail **(Photo I).** Cut the arc with a jigsaw and sand it smooth.

Join the side assemblies to the rails with a pair of connector bolts and cross dowels at each joint, according to the manufacturer's installation instructions **(Photo J).** Check the sofa frame to make sure it's square.

FRAMES AND OTTOMAN

The futon seat and backrest are simply frames that contain ½-in.-thick slats. The backrest side rails extend past the bottom rail to capture the seat frame (which is not as wide) inside. The frames are pinned together with clevis pins secured with cotter pins. The clevis serves as a pivot at each joint. Mill the frame parts to size; then cut a ¾-in.-wide × ½-in.-deep rabbet in the top inside edge of each front and back rail **(Photo K).** The ledges created by the rabbets will support the slats. Make the frame spreaders; then assemble the frames with the spreaders spaced as shown in **Photo L.**

The ottoman is built using the same basic techniques used to make the sofa frame and the seat and backrest frames. The main difference is that the ledges for the slats are milled directly into the front and back rail of the ottoman. Build the ottoman, milling the slats for it, the backrest and seat frames in the process. Sand and finish all the futon frame

Cut rabbets in the rails to support the ends of the slats in the backrest, seat and ottoman.

Assemble the frames for the seat and backrest, including the spreaders, using dowels and glue.

Once all of the parts are cut, but before the slats are installed, sand the wood to 150-grit and apply your finish.

Install the slats in the ottoman, backrest and seat by driving two screws at each slat end. Insert a spacer between slats for consistency.

Join the backrest frame and seat frame with a clevis pin inserted into guide holes at the ends of the frames. Secure with a cotter pin.

Loosen the rail-leg joints so you can fit the backrest/seat frames and rollers into the sofa frame, with the rollers aligned in their grooves. Retighten the screws at the leg/rail joints.

and ottoman parts **(Photo M).** I used a dark mahogany gel stain with three thin coats of tung oil as a topcoat.

Install the slats, spacing them on the ledges as shown. Use two 1¼-in. screws at each joint **(Photo N).**

PUTTING IT TOGETHER

Lay out drilling centerpoints for the clevis pins that join the seat frame and backrest frame; then make the connection **(Photo O).** Also plot out drilling points and mount the roller hardware in the ends of the backrest frame as shown in the drawing on p. 69. Loosen the connector bolts holding the sofa frame together and separate the side assemblies so you can fit the seat and backrest between the frame arms. Slip the rollers into the grooves; then tighten the connector bolts to draw the sofa frame together

(Photo P). Test the operation, making sure the seat rests solidly on the front rail of the sofa frame when the futon is set up as a couch. The seat and backrest should also be level and even with the top of the ottoman frame when the futon is converted to a bed.

Once everything is set, you may want to attach strips of mesh-style anti-skid carpet pad to the seat and backrest slats to minimize mattress movement.

Mark Johanson, writer
Mark Macemon, photography
Dan Cary, builder and photo production
Brad Classon, production assistance
Gabriel Graphics, illustration

Entertainment Storage Rack

Though relatively short-lived, the Arts and Crafts movement had a profound and long-lasting effect on American furniture design. The movement began around the turn of the 20th century and lasted only about 20 years. But today people are tripping over each other to collect these prized creations that emphasized clean lines, practical functionality and solid craftsmanship. Here's a chance to make your own piece of history and give it a very modern use.

Entertainment Storage Rack

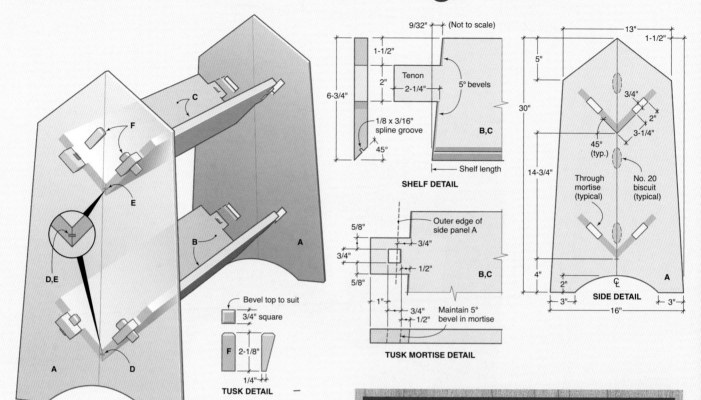

SHELF DETAIL

9/32" (Not to scale)

1-1/2"

6-3/4"

2"

Tenon
2-1/4"

5° bevels

1/8 x 3/16"
spline groove

45°

B,C

Shelf length

SIDE DETAIL

13"

1-1/2"

5"

30"

3/4"

2"

3-1/4"

45° (typ.)

14-3/4"

Through mortise (typical)

No. 20 biscuit (typical)

4"

2"

3"

C L

3"

16"

A

TUSK MORTISE DETAIL

5/8"

3/4"

5/8"

3/4"

1/2"

1"

3/4"

1/2"

Outer edge of side panel A

3/4"

Maintain 5° bevel in mortise

B,C

Bevel top to suit

3/4" square

F 2-1/8"

1/4"

TUSK DETAIL

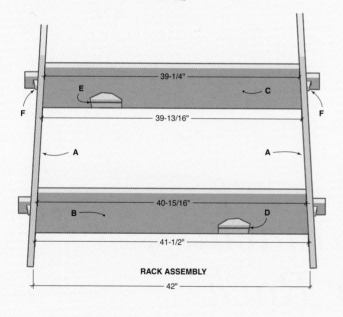

39-1/4"

E

C

39-13/16"

F

F

A

A

40-15/16"

B

D

41-1/2"

42"

RACK ASSEMBLY

Materials and Cutting List

Part/Description	No.	Size
A Sides	2	$\frac{3}{4} \times 16 \times 30$ in.
B Lower shelves	2	$\frac{3}{4} \times 6\frac{3}{4} \times 41\frac{1}{2}$ in.
C Upper shelves	2	$\frac{3}{4} \times 6\frac{3}{4} \times 39\frac{13}{16}$ in.
D Lower shelf spline	1	$\frac{1}{8} \times \frac{3}{8} \times 41\frac{1}{2}$ in.
E Upper shelf spline	1	$\frac{1}{8} \times \frac{3}{8} \times 39\frac{13}{16}$ in.
F Tusks	8	$\frac{3}{4} \times \frac{3}{4} \times 2\frac{1}{8}$ in.

All lumber is quartersawn white oak, with the exception of the splines, which are hardboard.

Shopping List

☐ 25 bf ⁴/₄ quartersawn white oak (surfaced to ³/₄ in.)

☐ 7 lineal ft. of ¹/₈ × ³/₈-in. tempered hardboard splines

☐ No. 20 plate-joining biscuits

☐ Yellow glue

☐ Brown mahogany wood stain

☐ Lacquer

All lumber dimensions are nominal.

This entertainment storage rack was inspired by mail-order furniture offered by such companies as Sears-Roebuck and Montgomery Ward. It features quartersawn white oak, a mainstay of the Arts and Crafts movement, and is sized to hold CDs, videos or hardcover books. It's a surprisingly simple project constructed from only eight boards (two for each shelf and two for each side). But solid joinery gives it the strength to last for many years, no matter how often you need to pop it apart to move it to a new location.

MILL YOUR LUMBER

Start by milling ¼ rough lumber to thickness. If the stock is wider than your jointer bed, remove the cutterhead guard and make one pass with the rough stock **(Photo A)**. Though generally you should always leave the guard on, this is one of the few times where it's OK to remove it. Because the join-

ter's cutterhead isn't as wide as the stock, a portion of the face will be left unsurfaced. Simply adjust the jointer's fence to the width of the uncut band and make a second pass. This process will leave a slight ridge that is easy to remove with a pass or two through the thickness planer. Repeat the process until the board has a relatively smooth face; then be sure to replace the guard.

Next, flip the lumber on edge, with the dressed face you just created against the jointer's fence, and surface one edge **(Photo B)**. After that, simply run the lumber through the thickness planer until you've milled the stock to the required ¾-in. thickness **(Photo C)**.

MAKE THE SIDES

To create the 16-in.-wide side panels, first edge-glue two 8-in.-wide (minimum) boards together using No. 20 biscuits and glue. Use cauls to keep the wood flat while clamping **(Photo D)**. Once the glue has dried to a rubbery consistency, scrape away the excess; then use a jigsaw to cut the panels to the pro-file shown in the drawing (p. 76).

Mark the location of the mortises and bore the rough openings with a drill press **(Photo E)**. Remove the waste from the mortises with a jigsaw **(Photo F)** or a sharp chisel.

Surface one face of your rough lumber. If the stock is wider than your jointer's bed, remove the guard and make multiple passes.

Replace the cutterhead guard, and surface one edge of your rough lumber. Remember to place the milled face you just created against the jointer's fence.

Run the boards (place the dressed face against the table) through the thickness planer until you reach the required ¾-in. thickness.

MAKE THE SHELVES

I chose a splined miter joint for the shelves because of its strength, simplicity and ease of clamping. Although the joinery may look intimidating, it's surprisingly easy to create.

First, set your table saw blade to 45 degrees and rip the shelf components to the required width **(Photo G)**. Even though the angle of the blade keeps the stock trapped, use featherboards to keep the wood tight against the table and the fence.

To cut the groove for the spline, leave the blade set to 45 degrees. Adjust the blade height so that the top edge of the blade is $9/16$ in. from the throat plate, and move the fence $1/8$ in. closer to the blade. Run the shelf components through the saw a second time,

with the beveled edge you just cut meeting the blade and the 90-degree edge against the fence **(Photo H)**.

Lay out the tenons as indicated in the drawing, and cut them using a jigsaw **(Photo I)**. Mark the anticipated locations for the tusk mortises (see drawing), but don't cut them out yet — you'll need to verify their locations as you test-fit the entire rack.

For the splines, I used $1/8 \times 3/8$-in. tempered hardboard stock **(Photo J)**.

I chose tempered hardboard for its stability. If you don't have access to presized stock, cut splines from a larger sheet of hardboard using a table saw.

When gluing the shelf components together, first apply a bead of glue to one of the spline grooves, and work the spline into place. Apply glue to the

Edge-join two boards to form the panels for the sides using No. 20 biscuits and glue. Use cauls to keep the wood aligned as the glue dries.

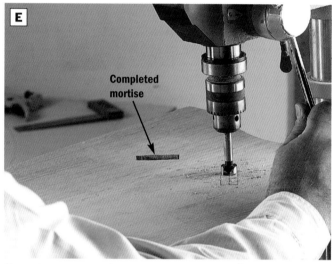

Clamp the side panels to the drill press table. Use a 3/4-in. Forstner bit to bore the mortises. Back up the workpiece with scrap to prevent tearout.

Clean away the waste from the shelf mortises with a jigsaw. You could also use a sharp chisel and mallet to clean out the waste.

Set the table saw blade to 45 degrees, attach the necessary featherboards, and rip the shelf components to the required 6¾-in. width.

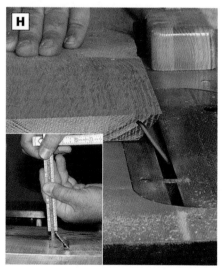

Leave the blade set at 45 degrees and set the blade height so that the teeth are 9/16 in. above the throat plate. Flip the shelf components around and cut the groove for the splines.

Carefully lay out the shelf tenon dimensions, and cut them to shape with a jigsaw. Remember to allow for the slope of the sides.

The $\frac{1}{8} \times \frac{3}{8}$-in. hardboard spline provides structural stability and locks the shelf components together as the glue dries.

Apply two or three coats of lacquer with an HVLP sprayer. Remember to lightly sand between coats. Work in a well-ventilated area, and wear an approved organic-vapor respirator.

opposite groove, and fit the two shelf halves together. To clamp the shelves together as they dry, merely place them upside down between bench dogs that are appropriately spaced to maintain the correct shelf angle — the spline itself, combined with the weight of the wood, effectively holds everything in proper alignment.

Once the glue has dried, test-fit the shelves and sides. Check the anticipated location of the tusk mortises, and make sure that no more than $\frac{1}{2}$ in. of the mortises will extend past the outer faces of the sides. (That way, as you drive the tusks into the mortises, they will draw the components tightly together and keep everything snug.) Then cut the tusk mortises as you did for the other mortises and remove the waste.

CUT THE TUSKS

Tusks are one of the unique components of Arts and Crafts furniture. Many different shapes were created over the years by leading crafters, and collectors can identify particular makers by the tusks' shape. Make your storage rack unique by designing your own tusk shape. Just be sure that the basic tusk form is $\frac{3}{4}$ in. square at the top and measures $2\frac{1}{8}$ in. in overall length and that the face opposite the storage rack side tapers to only $\frac{1}{4}$ in. wide at bottom, thus forming the simple wedge shape.

FIT AND FINISH

Test-fit the components. Make sure that everything fits snugly, with the tusks drawing the shelves tight to the sides. Then disassemble and sand all the components. Start with 80-grit paper; then use 150-grit and finally 220-grit. Wipe each piece with a tack rag after sanding.

To achieve the rich, warm brown color associated with Arts and Crafts furniture, I chose a brown mahogany oil-based dye stain. Functionally, dye stains differ from pigmented stains in that they appear more transparent.

To apply a dye stain, simply flood your workpiece with it and then wipe it all off. You can use a brush, rag, nylon scrub pad, sponge — in short, anything that will allow you to flood the stain and wipe it off before it dries. When using any solvent-based finishing materials, work in a well-ventilated work space, wear appropriate skin and breathing protection and always follow the manufacturer's directions.

I completed the project by spraying it with three coats of lacquer (Photo K). If you have access to a high-volume, low-pressure (HVLP) system, you'll get superior results with a minimum of overspray. Sand between coats with 600-grit paper, and buff the final coat with 0000 oil-free steel wool. Finally, reassemble the components and drive the tusks home. All that's left is to organize your CDs, videos and books and load the shelves.

Mike Berger, *writer*
Phil Leisenheimer and Mike Anderson, *photography*
Gabriel Graphics, *illustration*

Chapter 2

Outdoors

Easy Glider

When you're choosing a spot to enjoy a warm morning or quiet evening, you can't beat the gentle rhythmic motion of a glider. Combining the looks of a bench with the action of a rocker and a swing, gliders appeal to just about everyone. And because they don't require a structure above for support, gliders offer more placement flexibility than swings.

Easy Glider

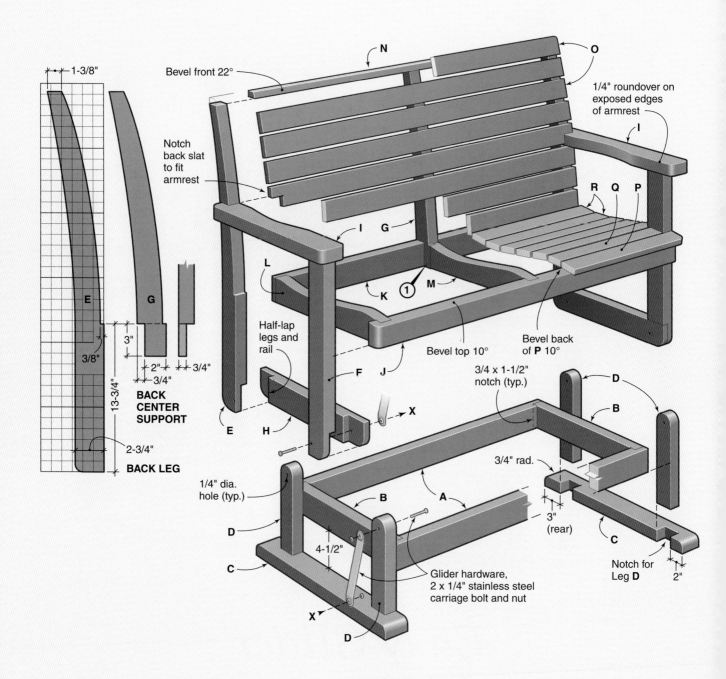

1-3/8"

Bevel front 22°

Notch back slat to fit armrest

N

O

1/4" roundover on exposed edges of armrest

I

R Q P

I G

L

K M

1

BACK CENTER SUPPORT

E

G

3"

3/8"

13-3/4"

2"

3/4"

3/4"

Half-lap legs and rail

Bevel top 10°

Bevel back of **P** 10°

2-3/4"

BACK LEG

F J

E H

X

3/4 x 1-1/2" notch (typ.)

D

B

3/4" rad.

3" (rear)

C

1/4" dia. hole (typ.)

B

A

D

C

4-1/2"

Glider hardware, 2 x 1/4" stainless steel carriage bolt and nut

Notch for Leg **D**

2"

X

D

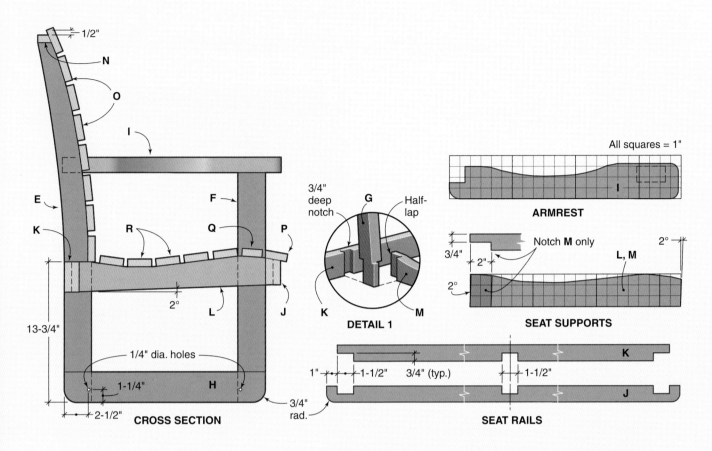

1/2"

N

O

I

E

F

K

R

Q

P

13-3/4"

2°

L

J

1/4" dia. holes

1-1/4"

H

2-1/2"

3/4" rad.

CROSS SECTION

3/4" deep notch

G

Half-lap

K

M

DETAIL 1

All squares = 1"

I

ARMREST

3/4"

2"

2°

Notch **M** only

L, M

2°

SEAT SUPPORTS

1"

1-1/2"

3/4" (typ.)

1-1/2"

K

J

SEAT RAILS

Shopping List

☐ 1×6 × 8-ft. poplar (4)

☐ 2×4 × 8-ft. poplar (6)

☐ 2×6 × 8-ft. poplar (1)

☐ Glider hardware (Rockler No. 58330; 1)

☐ 1¼-in. exterior-rated screws

☐ 1⅝-in. exterior-rated screws

☐ 2½-in. exterior-rated screws

☐ ¼ × 2-in. exterior-rated carriage bolts (8)

☐ ¼-in. exterior-rated locknuts (8)

☐ Exterior-grade wood glue

☐ Exterior satin or semigloss paint

Base Frame Cutting List

Part/Description		No.	Size
A	Front/back base rails	2	$1\frac{1}{2} \times 3 \times 39$ in.
B	Side base rails	2	$1\frac{1}{2} \times 3 \times 18\frac{1}{2}$ in.
C	Base feet	2	$1\frac{1}{2} \times 3 \times 25$ in.
D	Base legs	4	$1\frac{1}{2} \times 2\frac{3}{4} \times 12$ in.

Seat Frame Cutting List

Part/Description		No.	Size
E	Back legs	2	$1\frac{1}{2} \times 5\frac{1}{2} \times 35\frac{1}{4}$ in.
F	Front legs	2	$1\frac{1}{2} \times 2\frac{3}{4} \times 22\frac{1}{2}$ in.
G	Center back support	1	$1\frac{1}{2} \times 5\frac{1}{2} \times 24\frac{1}{2}$ in.
H	Side bottom rails	2	$1\frac{1}{2} \times 3 \times 20$ in.
I	Armrests	2	$1\frac{1}{2} \times 3\frac{1}{4} \times 21\frac{3}{4}$ in.
J	Front seat rail	1	$1\frac{1}{2} \times 2\frac{5}{8} \times 46\frac{1}{2}$ in.
K	Back seat rail	1	$1\frac{1}{2} \times 3 \times 44\frac{1}{2}$ in.
L	Side seat supports	2	$1\frac{1}{2} \times 3 \times 20$ in.
M	Center seat support	1	$1\frac{1}{2} \times 3 \times 20$ in.
N	Top crosspiece	1	$\frac{3}{4} \times 1\frac{3}{8} \times 47\frac{1}{2}$ in.

Seat Slats Cutting List

Part/Description		No.	Size
O	Back slats	8	$\frac{3}{4} \times 2\frac{1}{2} \times 47\frac{1}{2}$ in.
P	Front seat slat	1	$\frac{3}{4} \times 2\frac{1}{4} \times 47\frac{1}{2}$ in.
Q	Second seat slat	1	$\frac{3}{4} \times 2 \times 44\frac{1}{2}$ in.
R	Seat slats	5	$\frac{3}{4} \times 2\frac{3}{8} \times 47\frac{1}{2}$ in.

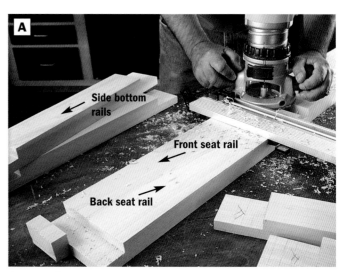

Side bottom rails

Front seat rail

Back seat rail

Use a straightedge to guide the router while cutting the rabbets and dadoes. Make several passes, lowering the router ⅛ to ¼ in. with each pass.

The most common glider designs incorporate a bench-style seat frame that rides on four swing arms attached to a base frame. Glider swing arms can be made of wood or metal. We used metal swing arms because they feature enclosed bearings for smooth operation and long life and were inexpensive and easy to install.

Building a glider isn't difficult. This design is intended to be attractive and comfortable but simple enough that anyone with basic woodworking skills can build it. I used dado and half-lap joinery for most of the connections and fastened the joints with exterior wood glue and deck screws. These joints are stronger than plain butt joints but are not difficult to create. I used a table saw and router for most of the milling operations, but you could achieve similar results with a circular saw.

All parts are cut from standard dimensional lumber (1×6s, 2×4s and 2×6s) available at most home centers. The seat slats are shorter than 4 ft. to allow the use of common 8-ft. boards. Because this glider was destined for a semiprotected porch location, we made it from poplar and applied exterior-grade paint. If you plan to place the glider outside, use a more weather-resistant lumber such as cedar, redwood, cypress or white oak.

CUT OUT THE PARTS

When milling the stock, first cut it to length; then rout any dadoes or rabbets and rip it to the final width or cut the shaped profiles. Next, cut the frame pieces to length. Note the 2-degree miter cuts on the ends of the three seat supports and the bottom of the center backrest.

Locate the rabbet and dado positions on each piece (see drawing, pp. 83-84). I used a router equipped with a ¾-in.-dia. straight bit to cut the dadoes and rabbets. Clamp matching parts together, making sure that the layout lines are aligned, and rout them

at the same time **(Photo A).** If you don't have a router, you can cut the dadoes and rabbets with a circular saw (see "Circular Saw Option," p. 86).

Once you've cut all the dadoes and rabbets, rip the straight pieces to their final widths. Rip a 10-degree bevel along the top edge of the front seat rail J **(Photo B)** and the back edge of the front seat slat P. Rip a 22-degree bevel along the front edge of the top crosspiece N.

Next, you'll need to cut the shaped pieces. I made hardboard templates **(Photo C)** first before drawing the curves on the actual stock. I transferred the pattern for each piece (see drawing) to a full-scale grid of 1-in. squares that I drew on paper.

Draw the patterns on the full-scale grids as they appear in the illustrations. Fasten the patterns to ¼-in. hardboard with spray adhesive and cut them out with a jigsaw. Sand the edges of the templates smooth and trace them onto the stock. Then cut out each piece with a jigsaw **(Photo D).**

Tip: To make cutting the stock easier, I placed a piece of rigid-foam insulation that is thicker than the maximum blade cutting depth under the workpiece. The foam supported the workpiece and waste, allowing me to stop and reposition during cuts without reclamping along the edge of the table.

After shaping the parts, clamp the matching pieces together and sand them so that they are identical.

Rip a 10-degree bevel along the top edge of the front seat rail J (pictured) and the back edge of the front seat slat P, and rip a 22-degree bevel along the front edge of the top crosspiece N.

Make templates for each shaped piece by transferring the drawings to a 1 × 1-in. grid adhered to hardboard. Then trace the template onto the workpiece.

Seat support

Maximum cutting depth

Cut the profiles with a jigsaw. Support the workpiece with 1½-in.-thick rigid-foam insulation. The foam and workpiece must be thicker than the maximum cutting depth of the blade (see inset).

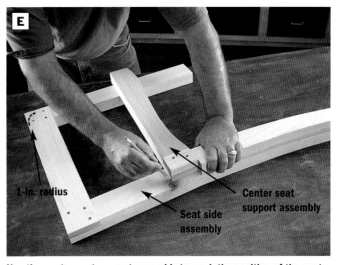

1-in. radius

Seat side assembly

Center seat support assembly

Use the center seat support assembly to mark the position of the seat supports on the seat side assemblies.

Sand all surfaces smooth and ease the edges — I used a ⅛-in. roundover bit on all edges that did not mate with other pieces.

ASSEMBLE THE FRAMES

Assemble the base frame first. Position the base sides in the rabbets cut in the base stretchers and fasten them with glue and 1⅝-in. screws. Then fasten the base legs in the notches of the base feet with glue and 2½-in. screws. Complete the base assembly by gluing and screwing the base sides to the base legs.

Assemble the seat frame by fastening the legs to the side bottom rails and the center seat support to the center back support with glue and 1¼-in. screws. Note: Keep the screws clear of the glider hardware bolt holes. Use the center seat support assembly to

locate the position of the side seat supports on the side assembly **(Photo E).** Attach the side seat supports to the side assemblies with glue and 2½-in. screws. Trim the bottom corners of the side assemblies to 1-in. radius.

Next, fasten the front and back rails to the center seat support assembly with glue and 2½-in. screws. Fasten the seat support assembly to the seat side assemblies with glue and 2½-in. screws **(Photo F).** Finish the seat frame by fastening the top crosspiece to the back legs and the armrests to the front and back legs.

Attach the slats to the seat frame with 1⅝-in. screws. Drill pilot holes and countersinks through the slats for each screw. Start with the bottom backrest slat and work up, leaving about ½ in. between slats.

Assemble the base and seat frames. Fasten the joints with exterior-rated glue and screws.

Mark the position of the armrests on the fourth back slat. Cut notches in the back slat to fit around the armrests.

Fasten the swing arms with ¼ × 2-in. galvanized or stainless steel carriage bolts and locknuts.

Circular saw option

If you don't have a router, a circular saw and chisel work well for cutting large rabbets and dadoes.

Circ saw option: Clamp identical pieces together and gang-cut each joint with a circular saw. Make several passes to remove the bulk of the waste material. Use a speed square as a saw guide.

Circ saw option: Break out the wood remaining between the kerfs with a hammer, and clean up the half-lap mortises with a sharp chisel. Hold the chisel flat to avoid digging deeper into the stock.

Notch the fourth slat around the armrests (**Photo G**). Fasten the remaining backrest slats and then move to the seat slats, starting at the front of the seat. The second slat must be cut to 44½ in. to fit between the front legs.

INSTALL THE GLIDER HARDWARE

Attaching the metal swing arms is the easiest step of this project. The manufacturer recommends installing the swing arms parallel to each other and perpendicular to the floor. However, we found that positioning the arms with the bottom bearings inside of the top bearings produced a much better gliding motion. We usually do not recommend deviating from manufacturer recommendations, but in this case we doubt the change will affect the life of the swing arms.

Drill a ¼-in.-dia. hole at each swing arm mounting position (see drawing). Fasten the swing arms with ¼ × 2-in. galvanized or stainless steel carriage bolts and locknuts (**Photo H**).

Before applying any finish, test the glider's operation. If everything is working properly, remove the hardware and apply exterior finish. I applied one coat of primer and three coats of exterior satin latex paint with an HVLP sprayer. If you chose a rot-resistant wood, you could apply exterior stain and sealer instead.

Vern Grassel, *writer*
Mark Macemon and Dan Cary, *photography*
Gabriel Graphics, *illustration*

Pinwheel Tree Bench

The idea of building a tree surround can leave a guy a little baffled. Most of the ones you see are the functional equivalent of eight or 10 chairs placed in a circle with their backs facing one another — a painfully antisocial arrangement! In addition, they tend to be complicated to build, with a lot of compound miter angles and some very tricky joinery. And what happens to the thing when the tree grows? Here's a better and friendlier solution.

Pinwheel Tree Bench

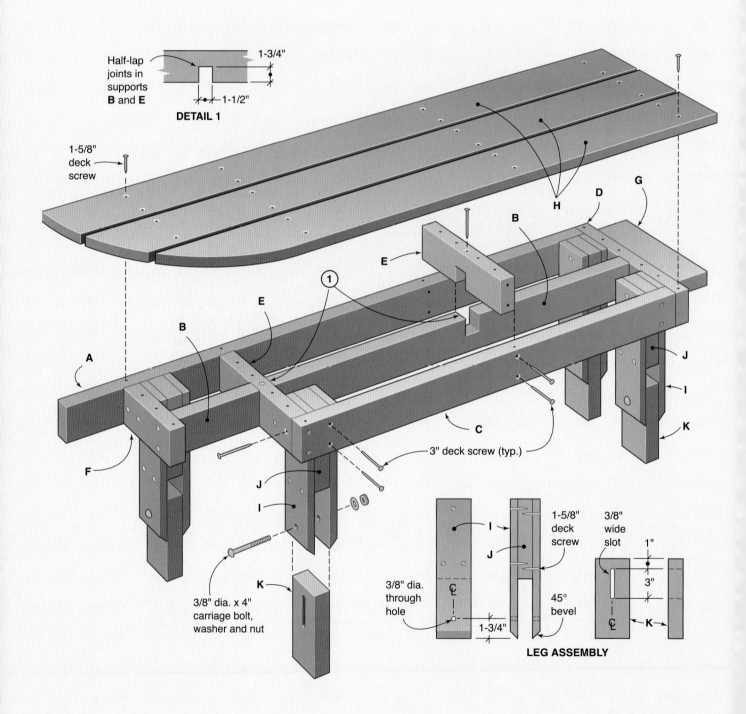

Half-lap joints in supports **B** and **E**

1-3/4"

1-1/2"

DETAIL 1

1-5/8" deck screw

1

A

B

C

D

E

E

F

G

H

I

J

J

K

B

3" deck screw (typ.)

3/8" dia. x 4" carriage bolt, washer and nut

K

3/8" dia. through hole

1-3/4"

I

J

1-5/8" deck screw

45° bevel

3/8" wide slot

1"

3"

K

LEG ASSEMBLY

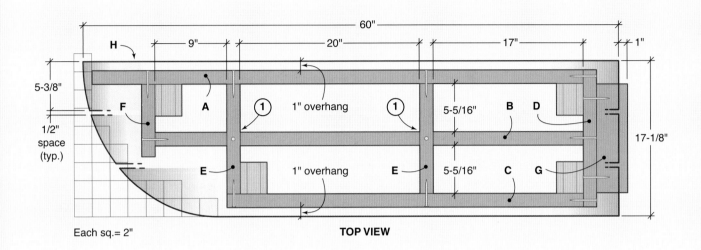

5-3/8"

1/2"
space
(typ.)

H

9"

20"

60"

17"

1"

F

A

1

1" overhang

1

5-5/16"

B

D

17-1/8"

E

1" overhang

E

5-5/16"

C

G

Each sq.= 2"

TOP VIEW

Shopping List

☐ 1×4 × 8-ft. cedar (6)

☐ 2×4 × 8-ft. cedar (11)

☐ ⁵⁄₄ × 6-in. × 10-ft. cedar decking (6)

☐ ³⁄₈ × 4-in. carriage bolts with washers and nuts (16)

☐ 1⁵⁄₈-in. deck screws (stainless steel or exterior-grade)

☐ 3-in. deck screws (stainless steel or exterior-grade)

☐ Polyurethane glue

☐ UV-resistant wood protectant (optional)

Material for four benches

All lumber dimensions are nominal.

Materials and Cutting List

Part/Description	No.	Size
A Seat supports	4	1½ × 3½ × 55 in.
B Seat supports	4	1½ × 3½ × 48 in.
C Seat supports	4	1½ × 3½ × 40 in.
D End supports	4	1½ × 3½ × 15⅛ in.
E Cross supports	8	1½ × 3½ × 12⅛ in.
F Cross supports	4	1½ × 3½ × 8 in.
G Cleats	4	1½ × 3½ × 12 in.
H Seat boards	12	1 × 5⅜ × 60 in.
I Outer legs	32	¾ × 3½ × 14 in.
J Inner fixed legs	16	1½ × 3½ × 8 in.
K Inner adjustable legs	16	1½ × 3½ × 8 in.

*All lumber is cedar.

Pinwheel Tree Bench: Instructions

My wife and I have a lovely elm tree in the back-yard, and she brought up the idea of building a tree bench around it. I scoffed at first, pointing out my three reasons why tree benches don't make sense. She thought about each reason carefully and offered solutions, and by the end of the conversation we'd come up with a plan that eliminated all of the problems.

This pinwheel tree bench has four "conversation corners" to allow two or three people to face each other when they're chatting. It's composed of four benches made mostly with butt joints. Because the benches are modular, you can spread them farther apart by loosening a few screws as the tree grows. And individually adjustable legs let you level the benches on almost any terrain.

The bench we built will wrap around a 2-ft.-dia. tree and still leave enough overhang at the end of each bench for a comfortable seat. If your tree is larger, adjust the plans by lengthening the benches. As a rule of thumb, multiply the diameter of the tree by 2.5 to find the minimum bench length, and add a bit to allow for growth. If possible, check standard deck board lengths with your lumber supplier before finalizing your plan so you can choose a bench length that minimizes waste.

SUPPORT FRAMES

To begin, cut the seat supports (8 in., 48 in. and 55 in.) to length from 2×4 cedar. You'll need one seat support of each length per bench, along with an end support, a short cross support and a pair of longer cross supports. Everything fits together with butt joints except for the half-lap joints between the middle seat support and the two longer cross supports.

Use a sliding compound miter saw set to cut 1¾ in. deep to make the half-lap notches (**Photo A**). It's easiest if you gang all of the middle seat supports together and then cut the notches in multiple passes. You could use a circular saw and straightedge, a table saw or a router if you don't have a sliding compound miter saw with adjustable cutting depth.

Cut the notches in the longer cross supports the same way; then make the half-lap joints. Reinforce each joint with polyurethane glue and a couple of 3-in. screws. (We used stainless steel deck screws that won't discolor the wood; **Photo B.**)

Next, attach the end supports and the front cross supports to the frame assemblies, squaring the frames

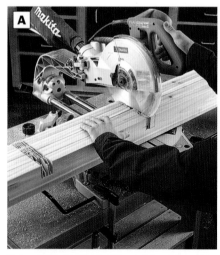

Cut notches for the half-lap joints with a sliding compound miter saw or a circular saw and straightedge. Gang similar parts together first. Clean out waste wood with a chisel.

Reinforce the half-lap joints with 3-in. screws (exterior-rated) and waterproof glue, such as polyurethane glue. Drill pilot holes when driving screws into edge grain.

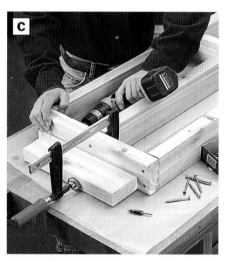

Attach a 2×4 cleat to the square end of each completed frame, flush with the top edges. The reveal of the cleat will fit under the over-hanging seat boards of the adjoining bench.

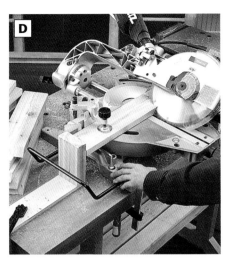

Bevel the bottom edges of the 1×4 outer leg components at 45 degrees to soften the appearance.

Drill a ⅜-in. hole for the carriage bolts through all three layers of each leg. The hole in the adjustable inner leg is used as a starter for routing the leveling slot.

Cut a ⅜-in.-wide × 3-in.-long slot in each adjustable leg. A router table simplifies the cutting job, but you'll still need to make two cuts, one from each face, to get through the 2×4 stock.

Install the inner adjustable legs with carriage bolts, nuts and washers. Then attach the completed leg assemblies to the bench frames using polyurethane glue and 3-in. screws.

Attach seat boards to the supports. Leave a 1-in. overhang on the front and back, and leave 1 in. of the end cleat exposed.

Make a template using the grid drawing on p. 89, and trace the curved profile onto the ends of the seat boards.

as you work. Then attach the outer seat supports to the frames and add a 2×4 cleat at the square end of each frame, flush with the top edges **(Photo C)**.

MAKE THE LEGS

The bench legs consist of two sections of 2×4 stock sandwiched between 14-in.-long 1×4s. The upper 2×4 is fixed between the 1×4 outer legs, flush with the tops. The lower 2×4 fits loosely into the gap between the two outer legs, and a 3-in.-long slot routed through it allows it to be adjusted up or down on a carriage bolt.

To make the leg units, first cut the outer leg sections to length from 1×4 cedar, and bevel one end of each outer leg at 45 degrees **(Photo D)**. Cut the

inner legs to length. Then join two outer legs and one inner fixed leg to make 16 leg assemblies. The tops and edges of the leg assemblies should all be flush, with the bevel placed at the bottom of each outer leg.

Insert an adjustable lower leg into each leg assembly so that it butts against the bottom of the inner fixed leg. Then drill a ⅜-in. guide hole centered side-to-side through all three leg parts, 1¾ in. up from the bottom of the outer leg bevel **(Photo E)**. The hole in the adjustable lower leg will be used as a starter hole for cutting the leveling slot.

Next, cut the slots in the lower legs on a router table with a ⅜-in. straight bit. The slots should start at the guide hole and stop 1 in. from the top edge of the leg. Because the leg is 1½ in. thick, we had to

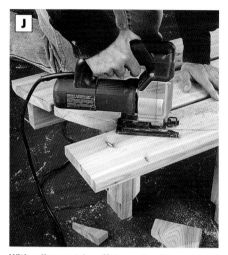

With a jigsaw, trim off the ends of the seat boards along the profile outline. For best results, cut just a hair outside the lines and then sand or file up to the line.

Adjust the benches until they are roughly level, then clamp them together. Make final adjustments, and then tighten the carriage bolts to secure the legs at the correct height. Finally, screw the benches together at the cleats.

rout the slot into one face and then flip the board and finish the cut from the other side **(Photo F).**

Attach the upper leg assemblies to the frame using polyurethane glue and 3-in. screws **(Photo G).** Then slide the lower legs into place and hand-tighten the nuts onto the carriage bolts to hold them there — use a washer on the nut end of the bolt.

MAKE THE SEATS

Once the legs are in place, cut the seat boards to the full 60-in. length from cedar decking. (Cut a 10-ft. board in half to make two boards.) Although they're billed as $\frac{5}{4} \times 6$-in. boards, the stock we found had actual dimensions of $1 \times 5\frac{3}{8}$ in.

Arrange three seat boards spaced $\frac{1}{2}$ in. apart on each frame assembly, and allow for a 1-in. overhang at the front and back edges. (Getting the overhang correct is more important than consistent gaps between boards, so make any compensations to the gaps, not the overhangs.) The seat boards should also overhang the end supports by $2\frac{1}{2}$ in., revealing 1 in. of the cleat **(Photo H).** Attach the seat boards to the supports using $1\frac{5}{8}$-in. deck screws.

When all the seat boards are attached, use the grid drawing shown on p. 89 as a guide to make a template for the profile. Trace the shape onto the seat boards and cut along the lines with a jigsaw **(Photos I and J).** Ease all the edges, and make sure all the screws are countersunk. If you want the benches to retain their cedar color, apply a coat or two of UV-resistant wood protectant.

SET UP THE BENCHES

Once you've completed the benches, simply arrange and level them around your tree. Start with all the adjustable inner legs fully raised into the gaps between the outer legs. If the benches are not level, find the high point of the assembly, and lower the other inner legs as needed to bring the seats above them up to level. You'll have about 3 in. to play with, which should be enough for most dips. If necessary, slip a couple of flat rocks into deeper dips.

When the seats are roughly level, clamp the seat boards to the cleat on the adjoining benches, making sure the benches fit together flush. Make final leveling adjustments; then tighten the nuts on the carriage bolts **(Photo K).** For added strength, run a couple of deck screws through the outer legs and into each adjustable leg after the benches have had a chance to settle.

Drive a few screws through the seat boards at the square end of each bench and into the cleats to pin the assembly together. As the tree grows, you can loosen these screws and shift the benches farther apart. And if the adjustable lower legs ever start to rot from ground contact, you can replace them. Just measure the distance from the bottom end of the damaged adjustable leg to the bottom of the inner fixed leg, cut a new 2×4 to that length, and glue and screw it in place — no need to bother cutting a slot.

Mark Johanson, *writer*

Mark Macemon, *photography*

Dan Cary, *photo production*

John Nadeau, Luke Rennie, *builders*

Gabriel Graphics, *illustration*

Summer Seat for Two

When it comes to comfortable outdoor seating, it's hard to beat an Adirondack chair. Unfortunately, many of us get to enjoy these relaxing chairs only seasonally, and finding room indoors for them during the winter can be a challenge. Keeping storage in mind, we developed a design that folds to 8 in. thick without sacrificing any of the classic Adirondack style, stability and comfort. If you prefer to relax alone or just want a more portable version, you can easily modify the dimensions of the two-seat chair (see "Summer Seating for One," p. 96).

Summer Seat for Two

Outside
5/16" x 2-3/4" SS bolt and locknut
1/4"   5/8"
7/8" dia.   7/8" dia.
5/16" SS washers

DETAIL 1 — PIVOT

F
1-1/2"
2"
3" SS screws (typical of framing)
Pivot hole
E
16"
F
G
7"
4-5/8"

BACKREST FRAME

1-1/2"
Pivot holes
21"
H
12-1/2"

FRONT LEG DETAILS

12"
2"
1-1/2" radius
5"
2"
I
3/4" radius
27"
Pivot hole
J
1-1/2"
1-1/2"
J
5"
18-1/8"
7/8"

ARM AND PIVOT BLOCK DETAILS

1"
Each square = 1"
1/4"
19"
1"
A
1-7/8"
15-3/16"
4-3/4"

REAR LEG PATTERN

Position of B
Cut one 12-1/4" section for seat support C
Frame member E fits between braces
Pivot hole
2-1/4"
1/4"-deep dadoes for braces D
A
2-1/4"
4-1/4"
1-1/2"
1-1/2"
2"
15-1/4"

REAR LEG DETAILS

16" radius
18-1/4"
18-1/4"
1-5/8" SS screws countersunk 1/4" (typical of slats)

Shopping List

☐ 1×4 × 8-ft. mahogany boards (10)

☐ 1×6 × 8-ft. mahogany board (1)

☐ 2×4 × 8-ft. mahogony boards (3)

☐ 2×6 × 8-ft. mahogany boards (2)

☐ 5/16 × 2 3/4-in. stainless steel bolts (6; available in Lee Valley set)

☐ 5/16-in. stainless steel locknuts (6) and washers (12)

☐ 3-in. stainless steel screws

☐ 1 5/8-in. stainless steel screws

☐ Polyurethane glue

Materials and Cuttng List

Part/Description		No.	Size
A	Back legs	2	$1\frac{1}{2} \times 5 \times 36$ in.
B	Front seat stretcher	1	$\frac{3}{4} \times 3\frac{1}{2} \times 44$ in.
C	Center seat support	1	$\frac{3}{4} \times 4\frac{1}{2} \times 12\frac{1}{4}$ in.
D	Bottom braces	2	$1\frac{1}{2} \times 4 \times 44\frac{1}{2}$ in.
E	Backrest supports	2	$1\frac{1}{2} \times 2 \times 32$ in.
F	Back crosspieces	2	$1\frac{1}{2} \times 2 \times 41$ in.
G	Backrest stop blocks	2	$1\frac{1}{2} \times 2 \times 3$ in.
H	Front legs	2	$1\frac{1}{2} \times 3 \times 21$ in.
I	Arms	2	$\frac{3}{4} \times 5 \times 27$ in.
J	Arm pivot blocks	4	$1\frac{1}{2} \times 2\frac{1}{2} \times 3$ in.
K	Seat slats	6	$\frac{3}{4} \times 3 \times 47$ in.
L	End and center back slats	3	$\frac{3}{4} \times 2 \times 32$ in.
M	Back slats	10	$\frac{3}{4} \times 3\frac{1}{2} \times 35$ in.

Cut 1½-in.-wide × ¼-in.-deep dadoes in the back legs using a router equipped with a straight bit and a straightedge guide.

To lay out the center seat support, lay the stock on top of one of the back legs. Hold the back edge of the stock flush with the leg's forward dado and its top edge. Then trace the profile onto the stock.

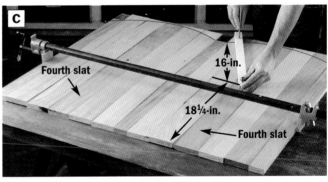

Center the pivot point of the compass 18¼ in. from the bottom edges of the fourth slats on the left and right of the backrest. Only the center 2-in. slat remains uncut.

Building this chair is not difficult, and you don't need a shop full of tools. In fact, you could get by with only a jigsaw, router and drill/driver, although a table saw, band saw and finish sander will produce more refined results.

Because the chair will likely spend the summer outdoors, use exterior-grade wood. The parts are designed to be made with stock-size lumber.

I splurged and opted for Honduras mahogany. It cost more and required some additional preparation, but it machined well and gave the chair a more formal finished appearance.

The stainless steel hardware came packaged as a set from Lee Valley Tools. The set contains more hardware than you'll need, but the price is less than it would cost to buy the necessary pieces individually.

CUTTING THE PARTS

Cut the parts to the dimensions shown in the cutting list (opposite); then use the scale drawings (opposite) to lay out the profiles and pivot-hole locations on the legs, pivot blocks and backrest supports.

Cut along the profile outlines with a jigsaw or band saw. Then drill ⅞-in.-dia. counterbore holes and ⁵⁄₁₆-in.-dia. pilot holes at each pivot-hole position. Pay close attention to the depths of the counterbore holes (see drawings). The locknut counterbores are drilled to a depth of ⅝ in., and the bolt head counterbores are drilled to a depth of ¼ in.

When the chair is in the upright position, the backrest supports fit between two braces that connect the back legs. The braces are secured in dadoes to provide the strength necessary to withstand the force of the backrest. Use a router to cut these dadoes (**Photo A**).

The width of the chair requires an additional support centered under the seat. Use one of the back legs as a template to lay out the center seat support (**Photo B**).

To draw the two arcs that give shape to the back-rest, make a 16-in.-radius compass from a scrap or use a piece of string. Clamp the back slats together on a work surface and draw two radii, one on each half of the backrest (**Photo C**). Cut along the radius line with a jigsaw, leaving the center slat uncut.

Drill screw countersinks and ⅛-in.-dia. pilot holes in all of the slats. The screwheads are countersunk ¼

Assemble the seat and backrest frames with polyurethane glue and 3-in. stainless steel screws. Use a damp rag to moisten the wood before gluing.

Tighten the bolts, washers and locknuts enough to create slight friction at each pivot point.

¼-in. spacer

Attach the end and center slats first. Next, fill in the five slats on each side, spacing them about ¼ in. apart.

Summer Seating for One

You can easily modify the plan to build a single-seat chair. Change the length of the parts as follows:
· Front seat stretcher (B): 23 in.
· Bottom braces (D): 23-½ in.
· Seat slats (K): 26 in.
· Back crosspieces (F): 20 in.
In addition, eliminate the center seat support (C), and use five back slats (M) between the two end back slats (L).

in. below the surface to enhance comfort when you sit in the chair — otherwise, you might burn yourself on a sun-heated screw. You could also cover the screw holes with plugs cut from the same wood used to make the chair.

Before assembling the chair, ease the edges with a router and ¼-in.-dia. roundover bit and then sand all surfaces smooth.

ASSEMBLING THE CHAIR

To fold up, the chair pivots on bolts that connect four main assemblies: the seat frame, the backrest frame, the arms and the front legs. First assemble the backrest frame and seat frame (Photo D). Then attach the pivot blocks to the arms.

Before bolting the assemblies together, apply an exterior finish to all parts. Finish is not required on exterior-grade lumber, but it will help preserve the wood color and extend the life of the chair. Without the finish, mahogany will age to a silver color within a year; with the finish, the color change takes longer. Apply an exterior stain every few years if you prefer to preserve the warm mahogany color.

After the finish has cured, connect each pivot point

with a ⁵⁄₁₆ × 2¾-in. bolt, two washers and one locknut contained in the hardware set. Connect the front legs to the seat frame first; then connect the arm assemblies to the front legs and backrest frame (Photo E). Tighten the bolts so there is some friction but the parts can still pivot.

The final step is to attach the seat and back slats. First attach the seat slats, working from front to back. Use ¼-in.-thick scraps as spacers between seat slats. Then attach the back slats (Photo F).

Setting up and folding up the chair are easier if you have a helper. To set up the chair, first position one person on each side. Place one hand on the middle of the backrest and one hand on the side of the armrest. Lift and tilt the backrest and lift the armrest until the back supports line up over the opening in the braces. Slide the backrest down between the braces until the stop blocks make contact with the back legs. Reverse the process to collapse the chair.

Dan Cary, *writer*
Mark Macemon and Dan Cary, *photography*
Gabriel Graphics, *illustration*

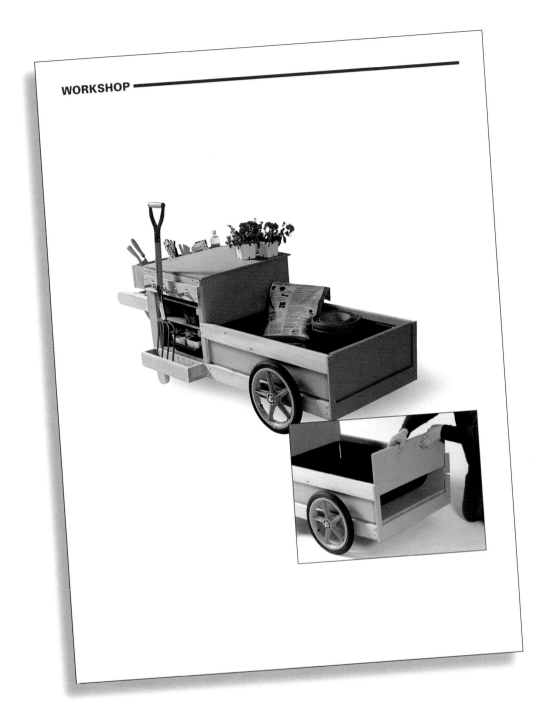

Gardening to Go

Gardening is fun, but who likes spending all day on their knees? Although some kneeling is necessary, it's better to work at a bench whenever possible. That's why we designed this portable workstation and cart. It goes wherever you need to work!

Gardening to Go

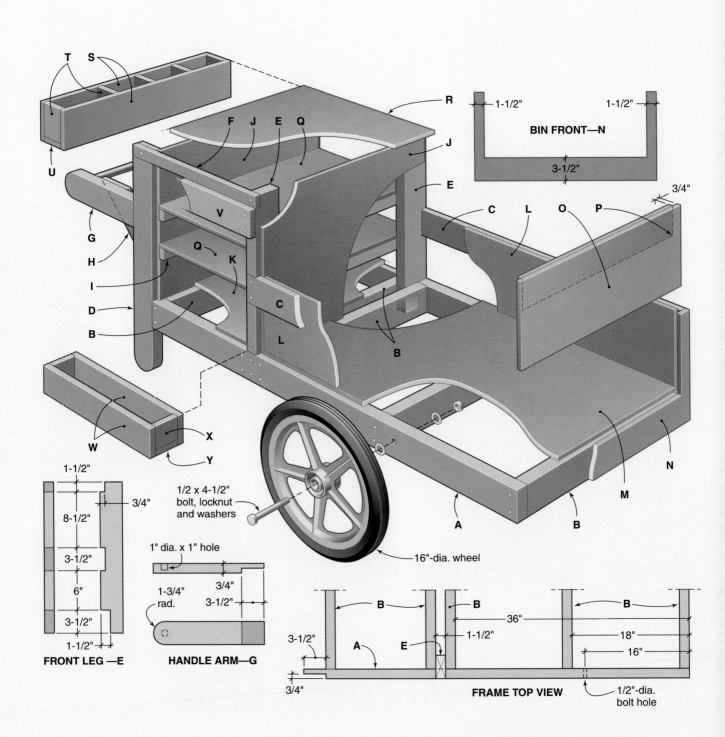

T
S
U

F J E Q
R
J
E

V

Q K

C
L

C
B
D
B

W
X
Y

BIN FRONT—N

1-1/2"   1-1/2"

3-1/2"

3/4"

C   L   O   P

B

N

M

A   B

16"-dia. wheel

1/2 x 4-1/2"
bolt, locknut
and washers

1-1/2"

8-1/2"   3/4"

3-1/2"

6"

3-1/2"

1-1/2"

FRONT LEG —E

1" dia. x 1" hole

3/4"

1-3/4"
rad.   3-1/2"

HANDLE ARM—G

B   B   B

36"

3-1/2"   1-1/2"   18"

A   E   16"

3/4"

FRAME TOP VIEW

1/2"-dia.
bolt hole

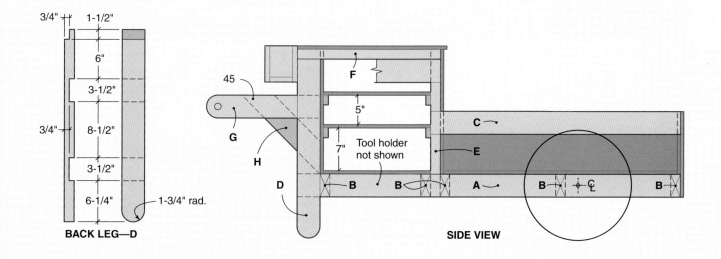

BACK LEG—D

3/4" 1-1/2"
6"
3-1/2"
3/4" 8-1/2"
3-1/2"
6-1/4" 1-3/4" rad.

45

G
H
D
B   B   A   B   C̸L   B

F
5"
Tool holder
not shown
7"
C
E

SIDE VIEW

Shopping List

- ☐ 2×4 × 8-ft. cedar (5)
- ☐ 1×4 × 8-ft. cedar (4)
- ☐ 1×6 × 8-ft. cedar (1)
- ☐ ½-in. × 4×8-ft. exterior plywood (1)
- ☐ ½-in. × 4×4-ft. exterior plywood (1)
- ☐ 16-in.-dia. wheels (2)
- ☐ 1-in.-dia. × 26-in. dowel
- ☐ ½ × 4½-in. exterior-grade bolts (2)
- ☐ ½-in. exterior-grade washers (4)
- ☐ ½-in. exterior-grade locknuts (2)
- ☐ Long-handle-tool brackets (4)
- ☐ 2½-in. exterior-grade screws
- ☐ 1¼-in. exterior-grade screws
- ☐ 1-in. exterior-grade screws
- ☐ 1½-in. exterior finish nails
- ☐ Polyurethane glue

Frame, cedar

Part/Description		No.	Size
A	Bottom rails	2	$1\frac{1}{2} \times 3\frac{1}{2} \times 59\frac{1}{2}$ in.
B	Bottom crosspieces	5	$1\frac{1}{2} \times 3\frac{1}{2} \times 24$ in.
C	Bin side rails	2	$\frac{3}{4} \times 3\frac{1}{2} \times 39$ in.
D	Back legs	2	$1\frac{1}{2} \times 3\frac{1}{2} \times 29\frac{1}{4}$ in.
E	Front legs	2	$1\frac{1}{2} \times 3\frac{1}{2} \times 23$ in.
F	Table crosspieces	2	$\frac{3}{4} \times 1\frac{1}{2} \times 22$ in.
G	Handle arms	2	$1\frac{1}{2} \times 3\frac{1}{2} \times 17\frac{1}{2}$ in.
H	Handle braces	2	$\frac{3}{4} \times 3\frac{1}{2} \times 17$ in.
I	Shelf supports	4	$\frac{3}{4} \times 1\frac{1}{2} \times 25\frac{1}{2}$ in.

Panels, ½-in. exterior plywood

J	Table sides	2	$\frac{1}{2} \times 19\frac{1}{2} \times 25\frac{1}{2}$ in.
K	Table bottom	1	$\frac{1}{2} \times 16\frac{1}{2} \times 27$ in.
L	Bin sides	2	$\frac{1}{2} \times 9 \times 36\frac{1}{2}$ in.
M	Bin bottom	1	$\frac{1}{2} \times 25\frac{1}{2} \times 37$ in.
N	Bin front	1	$\frac{1}{2} \times 13 \times 27$ in.
O	Bin gate	1	$\frac{1}{2} \times 9\frac{1}{2} \times 25\frac{1}{2}$ in.
P	Bin gate rail	1	$\frac{1}{2} \times 3\frac{1}{2} \times 24$ in.
Q	Shelves	2	$\frac{1}{2} \times 16\frac{1}{2} \times 27$ in.
R	Tabletop	1	$\frac{1}{2} \times 23 \times 28$ in.

Tool tray, cedar

S	Front/back	2	$\frac{3}{4} \times 5\frac{1}{2} \times 27$ in.
T	Sides/dividers	2	$\frac{3}{4} \times 3\frac{1}{2} \times 4\frac{3}{4}$ in.
U	Bottom	1	$\frac{3}{4} \times 3\frac{1}{2} \times 27$ in.

Long-handle-tool bracket, cedar

V	Upper tool support	1	$\frac{3}{4} \times 3\frac{1}{2} \times 21$ in.
W	Tool holder front/back	2	$\frac{3}{4} \times 3\frac{1}{2} \times 19\frac{1}{2}$ in.
X	Tool holder sides	2	$\frac{3}{4} \times 2\frac{3}{4} \times 3$ in.
Y	Tool holder bottom	1	$\frac{3}{4} \times 2 \times 19\frac{1}{2}$ in.

Gardening to Go: Instructions

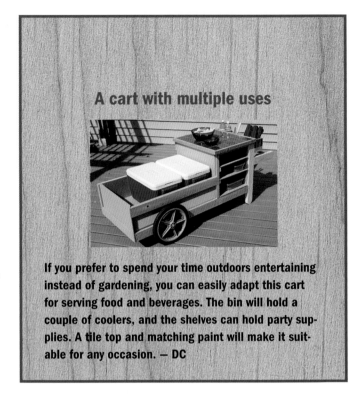

A cart with multiple uses

If you prefer to spend your time outdoors entertaining instead of gardening, you can easily adapt this cart for serving food and beverages. The bin will hold a couple of coolers, and the shelves can hold party supplies. A tile top and matching paint will make it suitable for any occasion. — DC

To give the design maximum appeal, I sought input from several gardeners. The bin features a front-lift gate and is sized to fit a 2 × 3-ft. utility mixing tub (available at most hardware stores and home centers). These tubs are great for mixing soil and are easy to clean. Hand tools, gloves, seed packets and a water bottle will fit in a divided tool tray, and a side-mounted bracket holds long-handle tools. The space under the tabletop can be left open for large pots and plants or divided with shelves to hold trays of seedlings.

I used cedar to make the frame, but any exterior-grade lumber will work. Use ½-in. exterior AC plywood for the panels, and fasten the parts with exterior-rated glue and exterior-grade screws (stainless steel, galvanized or coated). A circular saw and drill/driver are the only power tools you need. If you have a cordless saw and drill combo kit, you're all set.

ASSEMBLING THE FRAME

The frame is primarily built from 2×4s that are joined with half-lap joints. Use the drawing (p. 98-99) to lay out the locations of the half-lap joints on the bottom rails, front and back table legs and handles. Remove the bulk of the waste with a circular saw, and clean up the cuts with a chisel (**Photos A and B**).

Assemble the frame with exterior-rated glue and exterior-grade screws, starting with the bottom rails and bottom crosspieces to form the foundation of the cart. Next, attach the front and back table legs and the table crosspieces.

The handle is a 1-in.-dia. dowel that is held in place by the handle arms. Drill a 1-in.-dia. × 1-in.-deep hole in the inside face of each handle. Attach one handle arm and then attach the second arm with the rod positioned in the holes (**Photo C**). Finish the frame by attaching the diagonal handle braces.

To help preserve the color of the cedar, apply UV protective exterior sealer to the assembled frame, bin side rails and shelf supports.

SIDES, TOP AND SHELVES

All of the ½-in. plywood parts are rectangles except for the bin front. Use a circular saw and straightedge to cut each panel to size.

The U-shape bin front requires a few inside cuts. You can make the cuts with a jigsaw or small handsaw, but I used a circular saw. Secure the workpiece and reset the saw to its deepest cutting depth. This creates a more vertical cut at the front edge of the blade. First, plunge-cut the bottom cut line between the two side cut lines. To accomplish this, position the saw far enough in front of a side cut line so that the back of the blade will not cut through that line. With the saw resting on only the toe of the footplate, retract the blade guard, start the saw and slowly lower the blade through the panel (**Photo D**).

Once the blade has cut into the panel and the footplate is flat, push the saw forward to within ¼ in. of the opposite side line. Next, cut the side lines, working from the outside of the piece in to meet the bottom cut line. Finish cutting to the intersections of the lines with a handsaw.

Painting the panels will help prolong their life. (Only the glue used to make exterior plywood is water-resistant — the wood is not.) Sand the plywood

A

Clamp identical pieces (such as the two bottom rails) together and gang-cut each half-lap joint with a circular saw. Make several passes to remove the bulk of the waste material. Use a speed square as a saw guide.

B

Break out the wood remaining between the kerfs with a hammer, and clean up the half-lap mortises with a sharp chisel. Hold the chisel flat to avoid digging deeper into the soft cedar.

parts smooth and apply one coat of primer and two coats of exterior latex enamel (gloss or semigloss).

Attach the bin side rails to the bin sides and then attach the panels to the frame with 1¼-in. screws. Install the panels in the following order: table sides, table bottom, bin bottom, bin sides and bin front. Then attach the bin gate rail to the bin gate.

TOOL TRAYS AND TABLETOP

A tote box with a few dividers is designed to handle small items such as hand tools, seed packets,

gloves and a water bottle. It mounts on the back of the table.

Long-handle tools ride on the side of the cart, secured by manufactured tool brackets. These brackets are usually used to hang tools on garage walls, and they're available in different forms at most hardware stores. A small cedar tray is mounted to the base of the table to support the ends of the long handles and to keep the tools from sliding down.

Construct both trays from 1× cedar. Fasten the tray

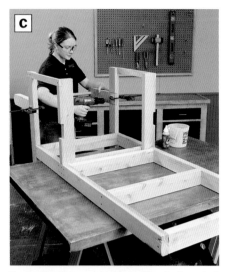

Fasten the frame members with exterior-rated glue and screws. Position the handle between the handle arms before securing.

Use the toe of the saw as the pivot point when executing the plunge cut. Watch the rear of the blade as you lower it into the panel, keeping it clear of the side cut line located behind the saw.

Assemble and attach the tool trays and upper tool support board with exterior screws.

Attach each wheel, placing one ½-in. washer between the wheel and the bottom rail and one ½-in. washer between the bottom rail and the locknut. Secure the locknut, but do not overtighten it.

parts with exterior-rated glue and 1½-in. exterior finish nails (**Photo E**). Mount the brackets on the upper tool support and attach it to the side of the table.

To attach the tabletop, drive four 1¼-in. screws through it, one at each corner. Then seal the screw heads with the same paint used on the plywood.

MOUNTING THE WHEELS

The final step is to add the wheels. I purchased 16-in.-dia. wheels. If your cart will cross rough terrain, I recommend upgrading to 20-in. wheels (available from the same source). In this case you will need to add 2 in. to the back leg length to keep the cart level.

Drill ½-in.-dia. holes through the base rails for the axle bolts. Slide ½-in.-dia. × 4½-in. exterior-grade

bolts through the wheels, place a ½-in.-dia. washer on each bolt and then insert the bolt through the hole in the base rail. Place another washer on the other side of the base rail, and secure the bolt with a ½-in. locknut (**Photo F**).

Your cart is now ready for the garden. Remember, it can get wet, but it isn't designed to stay wet. Store it in a location that permits it to dry, and it will make your gardening chores easier for years to come.

Dan Cary, *writer*
Larry Okrend and Dan Cary, *photography*
Gabriel Graphics, *illustration*

Swing on a String

If you have an empty porch begging for a swing, here is an extremely simple modular design that can be easily disassembled for storage in winter. This project is easier than you think, and the results are outstanding ... all the way to the relaxing evenings spent outdoors on your creation!

Swing on a String

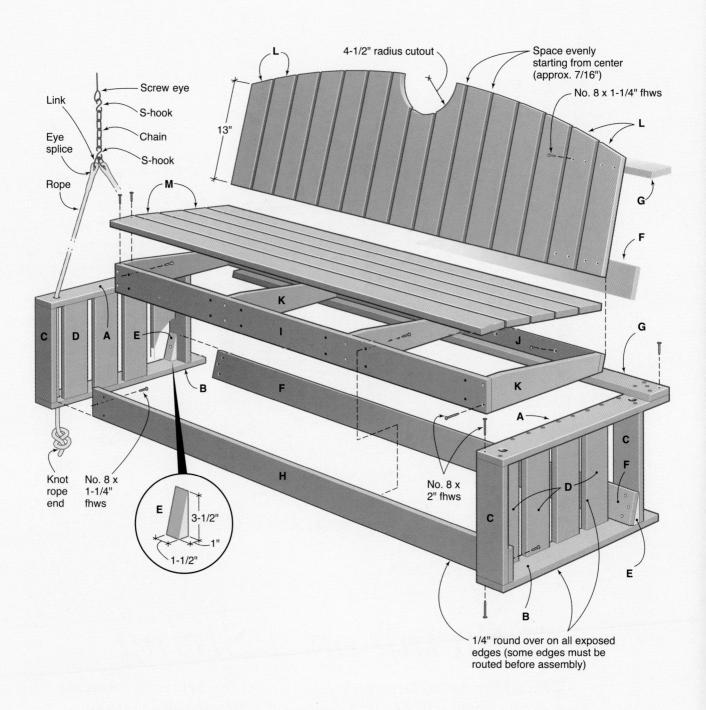

Screw eye

Link

S-hook

Eye splice

Chain

Rope

S-hook

4-1/2" radius cutout

Space evenly starting from center (approx. 7/16")

No. 8 x 1-1/4" fhws

L

L

13"

G

F

M

K

I

J

G

C D A E

B

F

K

A

C

F

Knot rope end

No. 8 x 1-1/4" fhws

H

No. 8 x 2" fhws

C D E

B

E

3-1/2"

1"

1-1/2"

1/4" round over on all exposed edges (some edges must be routed before assembly)

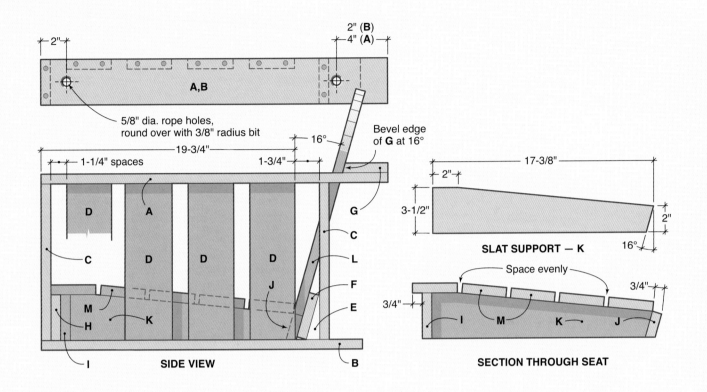

2" (B)
4" (A)

2"

A,B

5/8" dia. rope holes,
round over with 3/8" radius bit

19-3/4"

1-1/4" spaces

1-3/4"

16°

Bevel edge
of G at 16°

D   A

C   D   D   D

C

M   K

H

I

J

G

C

L

F

E

SIDE VIEW

B

17-3/8"

2"

3-1/2"

2"

16°

SLAT SUPPORT — K

Space evenly

3/4"

3/4"

I   M   K   J

SECTION THROUGH SEAT

Shopping List

☐ 120 linear ft. 1×4 pine

☐ 2×4 scrap

☐ No. 8 × 2-in. flathead wood screws (approx. 30)

☐ No. 8 × 1¼-in. flathead wood screws (approx. 160)

☐ ½-in. polypropylene three-strand twisted rope (4 lengths to fit)

☐ ⁵⁄₁₆-in. Grade 40 proof coil chain links (4)

☐ ³⁄₈ × 4½-in. lag-thread screw eyes (2)

☐ ⁵⁄₁₆-in. Grade 40 proof coil chain (2 sets to fit)

☐ ³⁄₈-in. S-hooks (4 to 6)

Sides Cutting List

Part/Description		No.	Size
A	Armrests	2	¾ × 3½ × 27 in.
B	Bottoms	2	¾ × 3½ × 25 in.
C	Fronts/backs	4	¾ × 3½ × 12 in.
D	Slats	8	¾ × 3½ × 12 in.
E	Wedges	2	1 × 1½ × 3½ in.

Framing Cutting List

F	Back stretcher	1	¾ × 3½ × 67 in.
G	Top stretcher	1	¾ × 3½ × 67 in.
H	Front stretcher	1	¾ × 3½ × 67 in.

Seat Frame Cutting List

I	Front seat stretcher	1	¾ × 3½ × 60 in.
J	Rear seat stretcher	1	¾ × 2 × 60 in.
K	Slat supports*	4	¾ × 3½ × 17⅜ in.

Slats Cutting List

L	Back slats**	15	¾ × 3½ × 18 in.
M	Seat slats	5	¾ × 3½ × 60 in.

All parts pine
*Tapered and angled parts, cut to fit; see drawing
**Back slats form an arc, see text and drawing

Except for two wedges, all of the parts can be made from 1×4s. Once you have the materials, it's easy to build this swing in a day. The time and material requirements are modest, and you'll need only a few tools including a miter saw, jigsaw and cordless drill driver. You can buy the required hardware at any hardware store or home center.

Preparing stock

I made this 5-ft. swing with about 100 linear feet of clear 1×4 pine (actual dimensions are $\frac{3}{4} \times 3\frac{1}{2}$ in.). If your swing will be exposed to the elements, you should use a rot-resistant wood such as cedar, redwood or white oak. With lesser-quality stock, such as No. 4 grade pine, you'll probably need twice as much wood. Pick through the pieces in the rack to find clear, straight boards. Avoid using boards with large or unsound knots. Be sure to buy at least 20 percent extra to allow for test cuts, waste and mistakes.

I use a sliding compound miter saw to make nearly all the cuts for this swing. To ensure square edges, make a few test cuts and adjust your saw before you begin. The sides (armrest frame) in particular require square cuts for the intersecting parts to align (see drawing). Be sure to use a sharp blade to prevent splintering.

Generally it's best to cut the longest pieces first because you'll use the cutoffs for the sides, back slats and other shorter pieces.

First, cut the two armrests (A) and bottoms (B). When you cut multiple pieces of the same length such as the side fronts/backs (C) and the side slats (D), you should set up a stop block on the saw to ensure consistent cuts.

Use a Forstner bit to bore the $\frac{5}{8}$-in.-dia. rope holes through the paired armrest tops and then through the paired bottoms. This reduces tearout and ensures that the holes are positioned correctly (see drawing). Rout the edges of the holes with a $\frac{3}{8}$-in. ball-bearing piloted roundover bit. Easing the edges will prevent the rope from fraying **(Photo A)**.

Armrest assembly

Simple butt-joint construction with screws makes this swing easy to build. It's important to bore clearance holes and pilot holes for the screws because the stock is relatively thin and prone to splitting. I use a countersink on a tapered drill bit (Fuller bit) to maximize holding power and set the screwheads flush or slightly below the surface.

You'll need to round over all exposed edges on the swing with a $\frac{1}{4}$-in. roundover bit. Some edges will not be accessible after assembly, so you should rout them first on a router table. Use a handheld router to round over the edges on the assembled swing.

A mistake I've made in the past is to build two identical side (armrest) assemblies. Be sure to make a left and right side. Also, use only coated or stainless steel deck screws for assembly — galvanized screws will stain the wood.

To ease the edges of the armrest rope holes, turn on the router and slowly tip the roundover bit into the hole.

Cut the wedges (E) with a miter box, but clamp an auxiliary fence to the saw's fence to support the 2×4 scrap piece.

To prevent splitting, bore screw holes before assembling. Note that there is a left- and a right-hand side.

Slat supports

After joining the sides and framing stretchers (see text), size the slat supports and then assemble the seat frame.

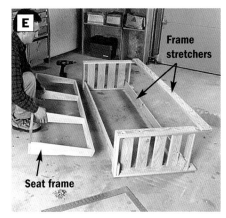

Frame stretchers

Seat frame

Install the seat frame between the front and back frame stretchers. Be sure the frame is square.

Determine the seat slat spacing by pushing the slats ¾ in. from the back; then measure the gap at the front and divide that figure by four.

Spacer

Use a spacer to position the slats; then working from the back to the front, install the slats with two screws driven into each support.

Screw each side frame together before adding slats. Then wedge the four slats into the frame, space them and fasten them with 2-in. screws. There must be at least 1¾ in. between the rear slat and the back of the frame. This allows enough room to insert the rear seat stretcher and wedge. After cutting the wedges **(see Photo B, drawing)** attach each with one screw.

SEAT FRAME ASSEMBLY

Once you've assembled the sides **(Photo C),** place them on the floor about 5 ft. apart (the width of the finished swing). First, prepare the top stretcher (G) by cutting the 16-degree bevel on one edge and rounding over the sharp edges on all of the framing stretchers (F, G, H). Then position the three stretchers, and using a framing square as a guide, screw the stretchers and sides together with three to five 1¼-in. screws in each joint.

The length of the tapered seat slat supports (K) is critical because the seat frame needs to fit snugly between the front stretcher (H) and the back stretcher (F). (Note that the slat support tails are cut at a 16-

degree angle — see drawing.) To determine the right length, make a test piece before you cut the work-pieces. Start with a piece that's a little long and trim small amounts off the end until it fits just right. Cut the tapers (see drawing) on the supports using an angle jig on a table saw, or use a jigsaw or a band saw.

Screw the seat frame together and set it into the existing framework **(Photos D and E).** Adjust as necessary to get a tight, level fit; then screw it in place. The bottom of the seat frame should be parallel with the bottom of the armrest. Now you can install the seat slats. Place the first slat ¾ in. from the back of the seat frame **(Photos F and G).**

SCRIBING THE ARC

The low-rise seat back creates the eye-catching line of the swing. It also helps to reduce the weight and places the center of gravity in a spot that allows the swing to glide smoothly. I install the first back slat in the center of the span. I make sure it's square and then fasten it with one screw in the top and one in bottom. Then I work toward each armrest using a

Scribe the arc on the seat back by bowing a piece of thin stock (see text). Anchor the ends and clamp the stock to the slats.

Use a 9-in.-dia. pot lid or a cardboard pattern to trace the decorative cutout on the three center slats.

Remove the back slats and make the cutout with a jigsaw or a band saw. Clamp the workpieces securely to the bench.

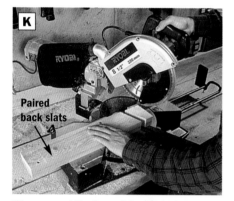

When you cut the tops of the back slats, decrease the cut angle for each slat by 2½ degrees as you move toward the center.

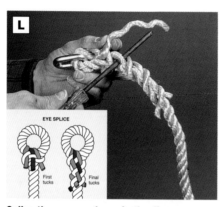

Splice the rope as shown in the diagram through a welded chain link.

Level the swing by adjusting the knots under the sides. The ropes should appear to be parallel.

$^{7}/_{16}$-in. spacer between the slats.

To scribe the arc, I rip a clear strip of wood that's about ¼ × ¾-in. × 10 ft. Then I bow it over the back of the swing and trace an arc (**Photo H**). (Note that this line is for reference only; it's not an exact cutting line.)

Next I use a 9-in.-dia. pot lid to trace the half-round decorative cutout in the center (**Photo I**). Then I remove all the back slats and cut the tops with a slide compound miter saw. I use the angle scale on the saw as a guide to make incremental angle changes on pairs of slats. This method works because the series of straight cuts (facets) creates the illusion of a curve.

The first angle, for the end slats, is about 18 degrees off perpendicular (72 degrees). Each successive cut, working toward the center, decreases by about 2½ degrees. The seventh cut is about 3 degrees off, and the center slat is at 90 degrees. To ensure symmetry, cut the slats in pairs starting with the two outside slats. Keep in mind that the cut angles will not always correspond exactly to the pencil line. However, by splitting the difference between the angle and the mark, you'll be able to create a smooth, graceful arc (**Photos J and K**).

Use a jigsaw or band saw to make the decorative cutout in the three center slats. After cutting and routing all of the back slats, you can install them. Center the middle slat and use a spacer to work toward the armrests.

I suspended my first swing with chain and I'll never do it again. Chain has no give and makes for a hard seat. On the other hand, rope acts like a shock absorber and is warm to the touch. That's why my favorite way to hang a swing is with three-strand rope braided onto a chain link (**Photo L**). I use ½-in.-dia. × 6-ft. lengths of rope and tie a knot under each armrest. This allows me to make adjustments as needed to hang the swing straight (**Photo M**).

If you want to apply a finish to your swing, a semi-transparent water-repellent deck stain works well, or you could paint it.

Raoul Hennin, *writer*
Bill King, Fuller Focus, *photography*
Gabriel Graphics, *illustration*

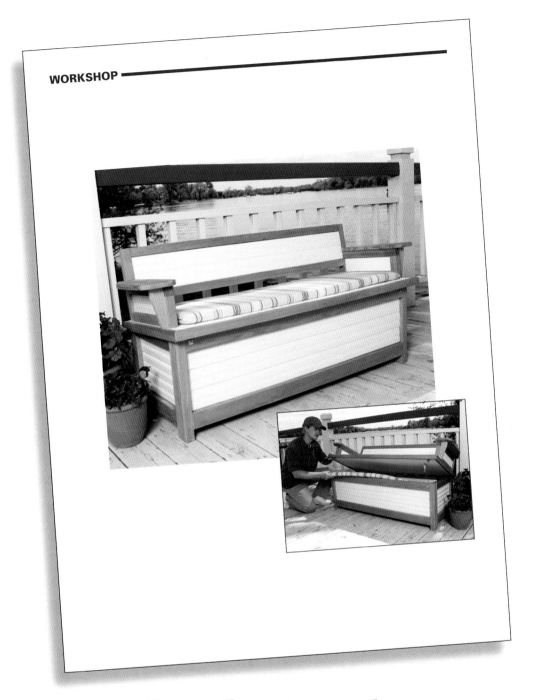

Deck Bench

If you've shopped for outdoor furniture lately, you may think that style and storage are mutually exclusive. You can find lots of attractive benches, but most storage options are just big boxes. So we decided to combine the good looks and comfort of a garden bench with the function of an outdoor storage box. The result is an innovative bench with clean deck styling, a low back perfect for leaning, and a sloped seat that provides comfort and flips up to reveal dry storage underneath. Add a cushion and you might even forget about all your other outdoor furniture.

Deck Bench

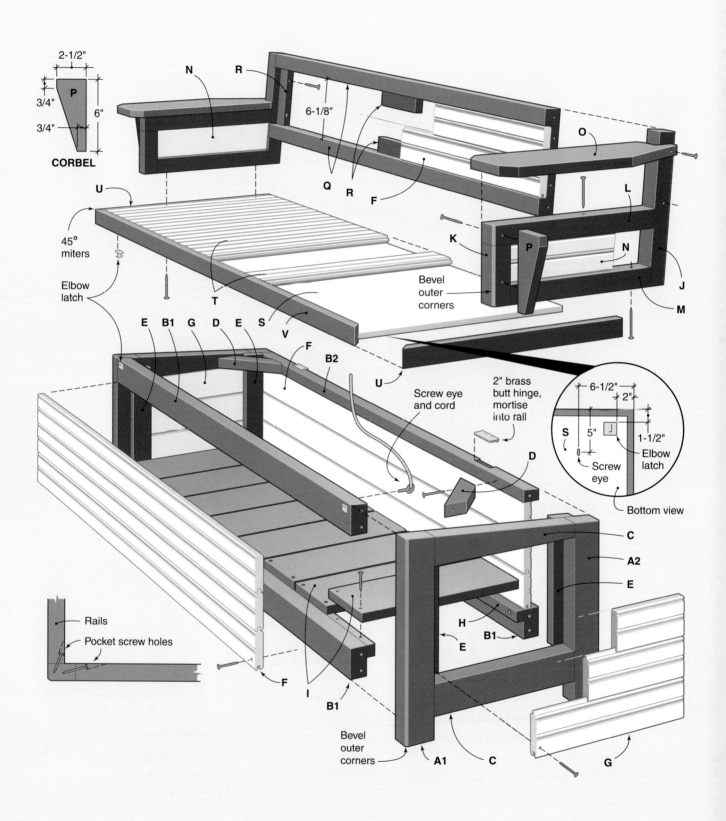

2-1/2"

P

3/4"

6"

3/4"

CORBEL

N

R

R

6-1/8"

O

Q

R

F

K

P

N

L

J

M

U

45°
miters

Elbow
latch

T

E B1 G D E S

V

F

B2

U

Screw eye
and cord

2" brass
butt hinge,
mortise
into rail

Bevel
outer
corners

6-1/2"

2"

S

5"

1-1/2"

Screw
eye

Elbow
latch

Bottom view

D

C

A2

E

Rails

Pocket screw holes

H

B1

E

F

I

B1

Bevel
outer
corners

A1

C

G

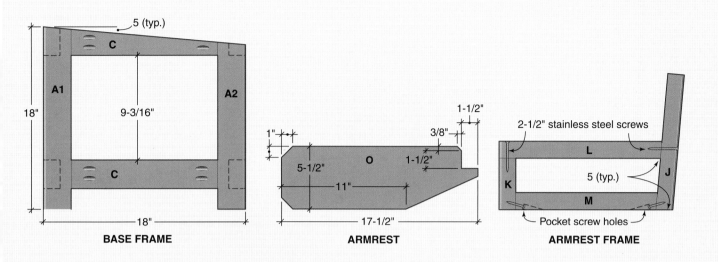

BASE FRAME   **ARMREST**   **ARMREST FRAME**

Shopping List

- [ ] 2×4 × 8-ft. cedar boards (4)
- [ ] 1×6 × 8-ft. cedar boards (3)
- [ ] ¾ × 3-in. × 8-ft. tongue-and-groove pine paneling (12)
- [ ] Elbow latches (Woodworker's Hardware part No. E1018B; 2)
- [ ] 2½ × 1¹⁷⁄₃₂-in. solid brass hinges (Rockler part No. 32782; 1 pair)
- [ ] ¼ × 1½-in. screw eyes (2)
- [ ] 2½-in. exterior pocket hole screws
- [ ] 2½-in. stainless steel screws
- [ ] 1⅝-in. stainless steel screws
- [ ] 1¼-in. galvanized brad nails
- [ ] ¼-in. × 3-ft. nylon cord
- [ ] Exterior primer (1 quart)
- [ ] Exterior acrylic/latex satin paint (1 quart)
- [ ] Polyurethane glue
- [ ] Exterior paintable latex caulk

Materials and Cutting List

Part	Description	No.	Size
A1	Front legs	2	1½ × 2½ × 16 in.
A2	Back legs	2	1½ × 2½ × 14¾ in.
B1	Front/back rails	3	1½ × 2½ × 48 in.
B2	Top back rail	1	1¼ × 1½ × 48 in.
C	Side rails	4	1½ × 2½ × 13 in.
D	Corner blocks	2	1¼ × 1½ × 7 in.
E	Base nailing strips	4	¾ × 2 × 10½ in.
F	Front/back panels	8	¾ × 3 × 48 in.
G	Side panels	6	¾ × 3 × 13 in.
H	Bottom slat supports	2	¾ × 1 × 48 in.
I	Bottom slats	8	¾ × 5½ × 15 in.
J	Backrest supports	2	1½ × 2½ × 12 in.
K	Armrest supports	2	1½ × 1½ × 4½ in.
L	Top armrest rail	2	1½ × 1½ × 14⅝ in.
M	Bottom armrest rail	2	1½ × 1½ × 12¾ in.
N	Armrest panels	2	¾ × 3 × 13⅛ in.
O	Armrests	2	¾ × 5½ × 17½ in.
P	Corbels	2	¾ × 2½ × 6 in.
Q	Backrest rails	2	1½ × 1½ × 48 in.
R	Backrest nailing strips	4	¾ × 1½ × 6 in.
S	Seat substrate	1	½ × 19¼ × 51½ in.
T	Seat boards	18	¾ × 3 × 19¼ in.
U	Side seat edge	2	¾ × 1½ × 20 in.
V	Front seat edge	1	¾ × 1½ × 52¾ in.

Don't let the refined looks fool you; this bench is surprisingly easy to build. The parts are machined from dimensional lumber, so a drill/driver, table saw and miter saw are the only tools you'll need. I used butt joints secured with polyurethane glue and pocket hole screws to assemble most of the frame connections, which means there are no complicated joints to cut.

BUILD THE FRAMES

I chose D-and-better-grade cedar for the framework. This nearly clear grade is available in my area at full service lumber centers. If you can't find it, substitute another exterior lumber.

Most of the frame pieces are square-cut to size, except for those that create the slope of the seat and backrest (see drawing, p. 110).

Tilt the table saw blade to 5 degrees and bevel-cut the top edge of the top front and back rails on a table saw. Cut the tapers in the top side rails on a table saw using a tapering jig **(Photo A).** Cut the top of each leg to a 5-degree angle to match the slope of the tapered top rails. (The specified length of each leg refers to the long edge.)

Assemble the base, backrest and armrest frames. I bored the pocket holes using a Kreg Jig **(Photos B and C).** Attach each base rail flush with the outside edges of the legs. Use two pocket hole screws (exterior-grade, coarse-thread, washer-head screws available from Kreg) at each 2½-in.-wide frame connection and one screw at the narrow 1½-in.-wide connections. Corner blocks attached to the top back corner joints reinforce the frame.

The storage compartment is protected from water but it is not airtight. The 1×6 slats that create the bottom of the base are spaced approximately ⅜ in. apart to provide a source of airflow. Attach the bottom slat supports and the base nailing strips to the base frame using 1⅝-in. stainless steel screws. Secure the bottom 1×6 slats with 1¼-in. brads.

I chamfered the outside vertical edges of the base frame legs and armrest assemblies with a router and

A

Taper the top side rail from 2½ in. to 1½ in. using a tapering jig on a table saw. Use a hold-down stick for safety.

B

Clamp each rail into the Kreg Jig drilling guide and bore pocket holes using the ⅜-in. step drill bit provided with the jig.

Apply polyurethane glue to the frame joints. Drive the 2½-in. pocket hole screws using the square-drive extension bit provided with the jig.

Drive 1¼-in. brad nails through the top and bottom panels in each opening, allowing the center panel to float.

Tap the seat boards together, clamping the previous seat board to prevent shifting. Secure every third seat panel with 1¼-in. brads driven at an angle.

chamfering bit. This optional step softens the edges and stylistically ties the frame to the panels, giving the bench a more finished appearance.

Complete the backrest frame assembly by connecting the two armrest assemblies to the backrest rails and attaching the backrest nailing strips. Before installing the panels, apply a clear water-base sealant to all cedar parts.

The two armrests and corbels are the only cedar parts left to make. Even though you won't attach them until after you've installed the panels, it is a good idea to make them now and finish them along with the frames.

The base and backrest frame openings are filled in with panels made from ¾ × 3-in. beaded tongue-and-groove pine boards (often used for wainscoting). The boards are installed with the tongue edge up to prevent water from collecting in the grooves. This leaves an exposed tongue at the top of each panel. Cut the tongue off of each of the top boards to create a flat top for each panel. Also cut the back edge of the armrest panel boards at a 5-degree angle to match the slope of the backrest.

Once you've cut the panel boards to size, you can sand, prime and paint all six sides of each board. Painting the panels before assembly seals all surfaces — and otherwise you'd have to mask the cedar parts before painting.

After the paint is dry, nail the base and backrest panels to the nailing strips (**Photo D**). Drill pilot holes and drive two screws through the bottom armrest rail and one screw through the top armrest rail to secure each armrest panel.

BUILD THE SEAT

The same tongue-and-groove paneling used on the frames conceals a solid exterior plywood substrate, providing a seamless cover for the contents of the bench.

Prime and paint all sides of the seat boards and plywood substrate; then attach the seat boards to the substrate (**Photo E**). Don't tap the tongue-and-groove boards tightly together; leave a slight gap to allow them to expand without buckling.

Next, attach the backrest assembly to the seat (**Photo F**) and attach the armrests and corbels to the armrest supports. Avoid splitting the armrests and corbels by drilling pilot holes before driving stainless steel screws through the edges.

Finish the seat by concealing the front and side seat edges with cedar edging mitered at the corners. Apply a bead of latex adhesive caulk along the edges of the seat, and secure the edging with brad nails. Leave the back edge exposed to allow water to drain off the seat. Fill the nail holes with exterior filler, and then touch up the paint.

CONNECT SEAT TO BASE

Attach the seat to the base with two 2½-in. brass hinges. Surface-mount the hinges (without mortises) under the back edge of the seat and 7 in. from the side.

Ask a helper or two to hold the seat over the base so that the hinge barrels clear the top back rail; then outline the hinge leaf. Cut ³⁄₁₆-in.-deep mortises into the top back rail for the hinges. Adjust the mortise depth so that when the seat is down its weight rests on the base frame members and not on the hinges.

Next, add the lid support cord and elbow latches. Install one screw eye along the inside of the front rail and a second screw eye under the seat. Tie one end of the cord to each screw eye. Adjust the cord length to stop the lid from tilting back more than 180 degrees. Finally, attach brass elbow catches under the front of the lid and to the face of the front top rail (**Photo G**). All that's left is to plump up the cushion and take a seat.

Dan Cary, *writer*
Mark Macemon, *photography*
Gabriel Graphics, *illustration*

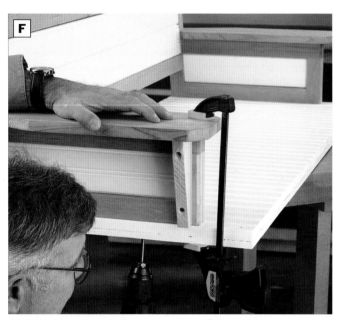

Drill pilot holes through the seat and drive 2½-in. stainless steel screws into the bottom armrest rails.

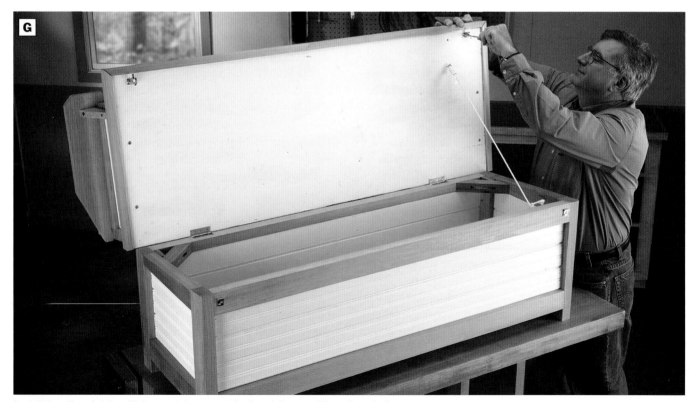

Install the elbow latches 48 in. apart to prevent the bench from accidentally swinging open.

Cedar Screen Door

No sound is quite as nostalgic as the slam of a traditional wooden screen door. When you hear it, you can't help but think of warm summer evenings and tall glasses of lemonade. The problem is, they just don't make 'em like they used to. Store-bought screen doors are often lightweight and unsubstantial, prone to warping and deterioration. And you could pay hundreds of dollars for a high-quality custom-built screen door. But why spend that much when you can build one for a fraction of the cost? This screen door is made from rot-resistant cedar and you can build it in a weekend. Its design allows easy modification to match almost any structure, and the parts are sturdy enough to withstand years of use.

Cedar Screen Door

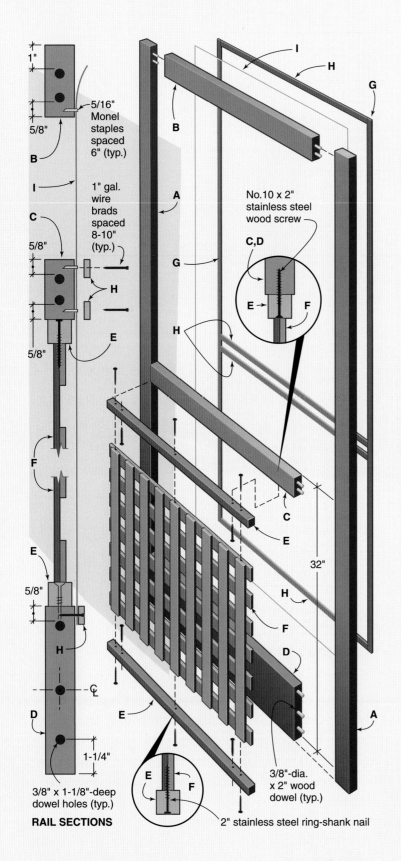

1"

5/8"

5/16" Monel staples spaced 6" (typ.)

B

I

1" gal. wire brads spaced 8-10" (typ.)

C

5/8"

H

E

5/8"

F

F

E

5/8"

H

D

C L

1-1/4"

3/8" x 1-1/8"-deep dowel holes (typ.)

RAIL SECTIONS

B

A

G

H

No.10 x 2" stainless steel wood screw

C,D

E → ← F

H

C

E

32"

H

F

D

E

F

3/8"-dia. x 2" wood dowel (typ.)

2" stainless steel ring-shank nail

I

H

G

A

Shopping List

- ☐ 8-ft. cedar 2×4 boards (3)
- ☐ 4-ft. cedar 2×8 board (1)
- ☐ ³/₈-in.-dia. × 2-in. wood dowels (14)
- ☐ No. 10 × 2-in. stainless steel wood screws (4)
- ☐ 2-in. stainless steel ring-shank nails (6)
- ☐ 1-in. galvanized wire brads (30)
- ☐ ⁵/₁₆-in. Monel staples
- ☐ 23 lineal ft. of screen molding
- ☐ 21 sf of 20×20-mesh fiberglass screening
- ☐ Rockler No. 49221 self-centering doweling jig
- ☐ Polyurethane glue

Materials and Cutting List

Part/Description		No.	Size
A	Stiles	2	$1\frac{1}{4} \times 2\frac{1}{2} \times 80$ in.
B	Top rail	1	$1\frac{1}{4} \times 3 \times 31$ in.
C	Middle rail	1	$1\frac{1}{4} \times 2\frac{1}{2} \times 31$ in.
D	Bottom rail	1	$1\frac{1}{4} \times 7 \times 31$ in.
E	Panel supports	2	$1 \times 1 \times 31$ in.
F	Lattice panel	1	$\frac{5}{8} \times 20\frac{1}{2} \times 31$ in.
G	Screen molding	2	$\frac{1}{4} \times \frac{3}{4} \times 71$ in.
H	Screen molding	4	$\frac{1}{4} \times \frac{3}{4} \times 31$ in.
I	Screening	1	36×80 in.

All wood parts are cedar.

Cedar Screen Door: Instructions

MILL THE PARTS

One of the nice features of this screen door is its simplicity — it's nothing more than a few lengths of dimensional lumber. Start with three 8-ft. cedar 2×4s and one 4-ft. cedar 2×8. (If your local lumber supplier doesn't stock 4-ft. dimensional lumber, just buy a standard 8-ft. length and save the extra wood for a future project.)

A few passes over the jointer and through the planer is all that's needed to mill the stock to the required size. Then cut the milled lumber to the lengths described in the cutting list, p. 116. Our door was made to fit our screened-in deck. Although this door is a common size, you should check your space requirements and make any adjustments before building.

ASSEMBLE THE FRAME

Another nice feature of this door is its simple joinery — a dozen or so ⅜-in.-dia. × 2-in. dowels hold it together. Start by temporarily clamping together the frame parts. Using a square, mark the locations of the dowel centers **(Photo A).** To ensure that you don't get the parts confused, also mark each joint with a reference letter.

After you've marked the dowel locations, you'll need to unclamp the frame and drill the necessary ⅜-in.-dia. × 1⅛-in. holes. To keep from drilling too deep, wrap a piece of tape around the drill bit at the appropriate depth to serve as a drilling index **(Photo B).**

It's critical to drill these holes accurately, so use a

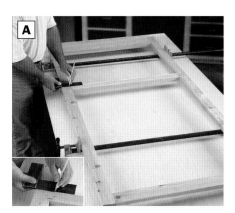

Clamp the rails and stiles together, and mark the location of the dowel centers on all adjoining parts.

When boring the dowel holes, use a doweling jig to keep the holes straight and true. A strip of tape around the drill bit serves as a depth gauge.

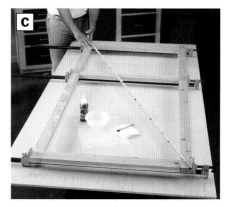

Following the glue manufacturer's directions, apply glue to the dowel holes and to the joint faces; then assemble and clamp. Check diagonal measurements to make sure the door is square.

After attaching the panel supports to the lattice, test-fit the panel by toe-screwing it to the door. Once you're sure it fits, remove it to add screening.

Slip a 2×4 under each end of the frame, and clamp the middle of the frame to the work surface. Staple the screening to the top and bottom rails; then release the clamps.

Staple the screening to the stiles and the middle rail. Keep the staples close to the inner edges of the rail and stile faces so that the screen molding will hide the staple heads.

Screen molding

After you've attached the screening to the door with staples, you'll need to conceal them with screen molding (also called retainer strip molding). Most building centers carry screen molding in a variety of profiles, so choose what best suits the look you desire. Because the strips of screen molding are so thin, they are highly susceptible to splitting, so drill pilot holes for the galvanized wire brads, and use extra care when tacking the strips in place.

Staple staining

Don't make the mistake of attaching the screening with ordinary steel staples — they will rust and leave ugly black stains on the cedar frame. Instead, use Monel staples, which are about 66 percent nickel and 33 percent copper. Arrow Fasteners (one maker of Monel staples) recommends using either $5/16$- or $3/8$-in. sizes — we used the $5/16$-in. variety. Monel staples can be hard to find, and you may have to special-order them. A box of 1,250 staples costs $8 to $15.

Attach screen molding to the frame to conceal the staples. Use 1-in. galvanized wire brads, and set the heads with a nail set.

nails for each support, and predrill all nail holes to prevent splitting the narrow latticework. Check the fit by temporarily attaching the assembled panel to the door frame with four 2-in. stainless steel wood screws (**Photo D**). Then remove the panel in preparation for screening.

Once the glue has cured, apply an outdoor-rated stain or finish of your choice — we used Natural Choice transparent finish from Okon.

ATTACH THE SCREENING

Allow a few days for the stain to dry and for the door to acclimate to its environment. This will prevent the door from warping after the screen is attached.

Before you add screening, remove the lattice panel to allow the frame more flexibility. Lay the door flat and slip a 2×4 under each end of the frame; then clamp the middle of the frame to the work surface, thus bowing the entire assembly.

Next, cut the screening to length (allow a few extra inches), and staple it every 6 in. to the top and bottom rails (**Photo E**). Then release the clamps — as the frame straightens out, it will stretch the screening taut. Finally, staple the screening every 6 in. to the stiles and middle rail (**Photo F**). As you work, try to place the staples close to the inner edge of the rail and stile faces.

Once you've attached the screening, conceal the staples with strips of decorative screen molding fastened with 1-in. galvanized wire brads spaced every 8 to 10 in. (**Photo G**). Then trim away any excess screening with a utility knife. All that's left is to choose hinges and handles. Classic brass or rustic black hardware would look equally at home on this traditional-style door.

Mike Berger, *writer*
Mark Macemon and Mike Anderson, *photography*
Gabriel Graphics, *illustration*

self-centering doweling jig such as Rockler's No. 49221. If you've never used a doweling jig before, you'll be surprised at how simple it makes this process. To accommodate drill bits for multiple dowel diameters, holes of various sizes run along the top of the jig, and index marks along the jig's body align with the desired hole location. When you tighten the screw, each side of the jig closes in equally, leaving the drilling hole exactly centered over the width of the stock.

To assemble the frame, apply polyurethane glue to the dowel holes in each of the rails; then insert the dowels. Next, apply glue to the dowel holes and to the joint surfaces of the stiles and clamp the assembly. As you work, tighten each clamp slowly so the workpieces are drawn together uniformly. Double-check that the frame is square by measuring from corner to corner (**Photo C**).

To assemble the lattice panel, use 2-in. stainless steel ring-shank nails to attach a 31-in. panel support to both the top and bottom of the lattice. Use three

118

Deck Bench and Planter

What's the point of creating a beautiful outdoor living space unless you look forward to spending time there? Even the most well-built deck can seem stark and uninviting if it lacks accessories that add visual interest and character. Building a matching bench and planter can make a deck seem more coordinated, comfortable and appealing. This bench and planter can be completed in an afternoon and require only basic woodworking skills. We used dimensional cedar for both projects, but any rot-resistant lumber (such as redwood, mahogany, teak or even pressure-treated pine) would work, and the only tools necessary are a circular saw, a jigsaw, a drill/driver and a sander.

Deck Bench and Planter

DECK BENCH

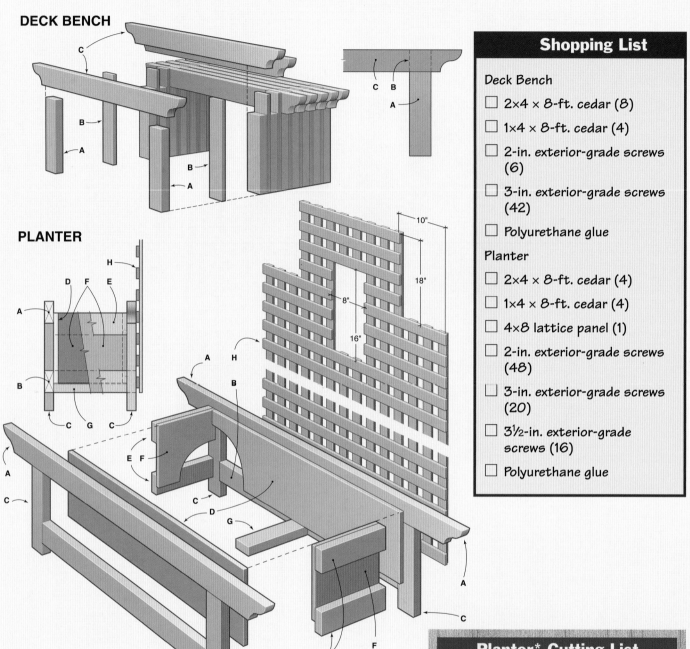

PLANTER

Shopping List

Deck Bench

☐ 2×4 × 8-ft. cedar (8)

☐ 1×4 × 8-ft. cedar (4)

☐ 2-in. exterior-grade screws (6)

☐ 3-in. exterior-grade screws (42)

☐ Polyurethane glue

Planter

☐ 2×4 × 8-ft. cedar (4)

☐ 1×4 × 8-ft. cedar (4)

☐ 4×8 lattice panel (1)

☐ 2-in. exterior-grade screws (48)

☐ 3-in. exterior-grade screws (20)

☐ 3½-in. exterior-grade screws (16)

☐ Polyurethane glue

Deck Bench* Cutting List

Part	Description	No.	Size
A	Legs	16	2×4 × 13½ in.
B	Spacers	14	1×4 × 17 in.
C	Seat Slats	8	2×4 × 48 in.

*All parts made from dimensional lumber

Planter* Cutting List

Part	Description	No.	Size
A	Top rails	2	2×4 × 76 in.
B	Bottom rails	2	2×4 × 48 in.
C	Legs	4	2×4 × 14 in.
D	Front/back panels	2	1×12 × 50½ in.
E	Side rails	4	2×4 × 12 in.
F	Side panels	2	1×12 × 12 in.
G	Bottom cross-brace	1	2×4 × 12 in.
H	Lattice panel	1	48 × 86 in.

*All parts made from dimensional lumber

Deck Bench and Planter: Instructions

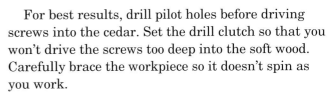

For best results, drill pilot holes before driving screws into the cedar. Set the drill clutch so that you won't drive the screws too deep into the soft wood. Carefully brace the workpiece so it doesn't spin as you work.

Repeat these steps, alternating legs and spacers, until you've attached all of the pieces for each side **(Photo A);** then clamp the assembled bench sides until the glue cures.

To build the seat, cut the slats (C) to length; then use a jigsaw to cut a decorative profile on the ends **(Photo B).** To keep the board ends uniform, use the cutoff from the first decorative end as a pattern, and trace the design onto the other board ends.

Next, apply glue to the pockets created by the alternating legs and spacers of the side panels, and drop the seat slats into place **(Photo C).** Clamp the

BUILDING THE BENCH

To start the bench, first cut the 2×4 legs (A) and 1×4 spacers (B) to length as indicated in the cutting list. Assemble the sides by alternating 2×4 legs and 1×4 spacers. Start with one leg piece, apply waterproof glue (such as polyurethane glue) to one face, and use three 2-in. exterior-rated screws to fasten it to one of the 1×4 spacers. Use 3-in. screws for subsequent pieces.

Use 3-in. exterior-rated screws and polyurethane glue to fasten the series of legs and spacers. Use three screws for each leg, and firmly clamp each side assembly as the glue cures.

Use a jigsaw to cut a decorative profile on each end of the seat slats.

Apply glue to the pockets formed by the legs and spacers; then drop the seat slats into the pockets.

Clamp the seat assembly as the glue cures; then sand the entire assembly smooth.

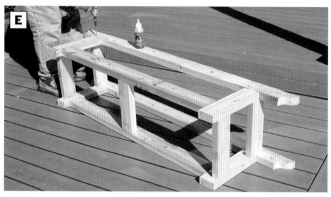

To assemble the framework for the planter, glue and screw the 2×4 sections together. Use 3-in. screws for all face-screwing applications and 3½-in. screws for toe-screwing applications.

Use 2-in. screws to fasten the interior cedar panels to the inside of the framework. Be sure to drill pilot holes to keep the cedar from splitting.

With a jigsaw, cut an opening in the center of the lattice. You can modify the silhouette of the panel to suit your taste.

Use 2-in. screws to fasten the lattice to the back of the planter. Drive six screws into the bottom rail and six into the top rail.

assembly and let the glue cure **(Photo D).** Don't try to wipe away glue squeezeout; instead, let the excess adhesive cure and then shave it off with a sharp chisel. Finally, use a belt sander (or other power sander) equipped with 120-grit paper to sand the sides and top smooth.

MAKING THE PLANTER

Unlike traditional planters designed to hold soil, this one is made to accommodate plastic containers as large as 10¼-in. dia. × 13 in. high. Besides preventing the wood from rotting as a result of constant contact with soil and water, this design makes gardening easier — instead of one large trough of soil, it holds pots that can be lifted out separately.

To build the planter, first cut all of the 2×4 parts to length as indicated in the cutting list, and cut the decorative profiles for the top rails (A) as you did for the bench. Use polyurethane glue and 3-in. exterior-rated screws to fasten the side rails (E) to the legs (C). Use glue and 3-in. screws to attach the top rails to the upper side rails **(Photo E).** Then from beneath, drive 3½-in. screws to toe-screw through the legs and into the top rails.

Using 3½-in. screws and glue, toe-screw the bottom rails (B) to the legs; then use 3-in. screws to face-screw the bottom cross-brace (G) between the bottom rails. Cut the 1×12 cedar side inner panels (F) to length, and use 2-in. screws to fasten them in place **(Photo F).** Cedar boards can split easily, so be sure to drill pilot holes before sinking the screws. Use three screws at the top and bottom of each side panel and six screws each at the top and bottom of the front and back panels (D).

Cut the cedar lattice panel (H) to size **(Photo G),** and fasten it to the back of the planter box **(Photo H)** with glue and 2-in. screws (six driven into the bottom rail and six into the top rail). Firmly clamp the lattice in place until the glue cures; then fill the planter with your favorite climbing plants.

Mike Berger, *writer*
Scott Jacobson and Mike Anderson, *photography*
Gabriel Graphics, *illustration*

Garden Obelisk

When your planting is done and your garden is filling in, consider accenting the vegetation with an obelisk. Typically constructed of wood lattice, a garden obelisk is basically a free-standing trellis. When situated near climbing plants such as a clematis or sweet pea, the obelisk showcases the vine and acts as a striking focal point for the landscape. To give our obelisk a unique flair, we included ½-in. copper pipe, which will develop an appealing patina over time. We topped it off with a manufactured post cap sized to fit a 4×4 post. The cap has a copper-clad peak to match the pipe, but you could make the peak match existing caps on your fence or deck.

Garden Obelisk

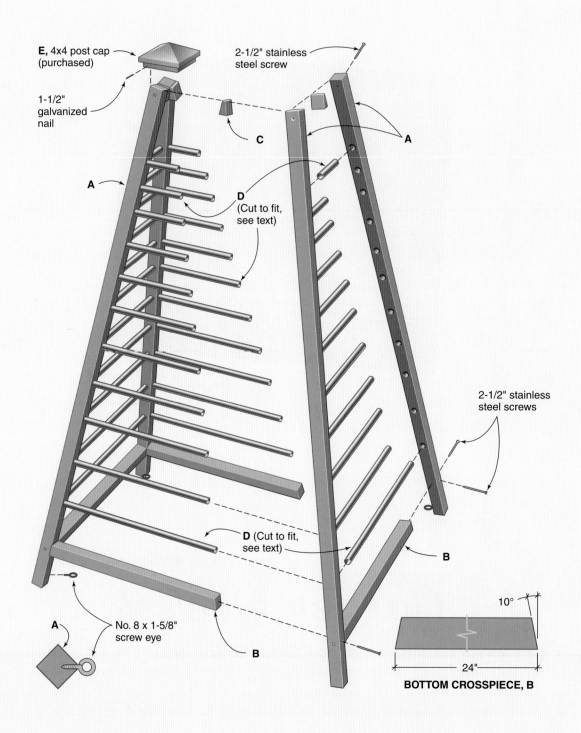

E, 4x4 post cap (purchased)

1-1/2" galvanized nail

2-1/2" stainless steel screw

C

A

A

D (Cut to fit, see text)

D (Cut to fit, see text)

2-1/2" stainless steel screws

B

B

A

No. 8 x 1-5/8" screw eye

B

10°

24"

BOTTOM CROSSPIECE, B

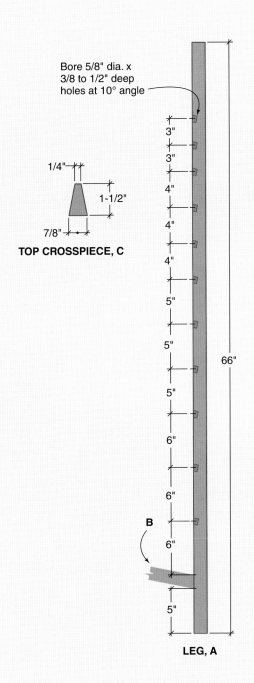

Bore 5/8" dia. x
3/8 to 1/2" deep
holes at 10° angle

3"

3"

4"

4"

4"

5"

5"

5"

6"

6"

B

6"

5"

66"

LEG, A

1/4"

1-1/2"

7/8"

TOP CROSSPIECE, C

Shopping List

- ☐ (4) 2 × 2-in. × 8-ft. cedar boards
- ☐ (5) ½-in.-dia. × 8-ft. copper pipes
- ☐ (1) 4×4 manufactured post cap
- ☐ 2½-in. stainless steel screws
- ☐ (4) No. 8 × 1⅝-in. screw eyes
- ☐ Polyurethane glue
- ☐ Exterior stain/sealer
- ☐ 1½-in. galvanized finish nails

Materials and Cutting List

Part/Description		No.	Size
A	Legs	4	$1\frac{1}{2} \times 1\frac{1}{2} \times 66$ in.
B	Bottom crosspieces	4	$1\frac{1}{2} \times 1\frac{1}{2} \times 24$ in.
C	Top crosspieces	4	$1\frac{1}{2} \times 1\frac{1}{2} \times \frac{7}{8}$ in.
D	Copper pipes	44	Cut to fit
E	Top cap	1	4×4 post cap

Note: All lumber is cedar.

MATERIAL PREPARATION

Begin by cutting the legs to length; then mark the inside faces. Next, mark the pipe-hole locations on the inside faces of each leg **(Photo A).** Marking all four legs at one time helps ensure that the pipes will be parallel when you assemble the pieces. The spacing of the tubing is graduated, beginning with 6-in. spacing at the bottom and finishing with 3-in. spacing at the top.

The holes for the pipes need to be drilled at a slight angle, about 10 degrees. I made a drill guide out of scrap ¾-in. plywood to help establish the angle and keep the holes centered on the leg. After drilling a ⅝-in. guide hole centered across the width of the

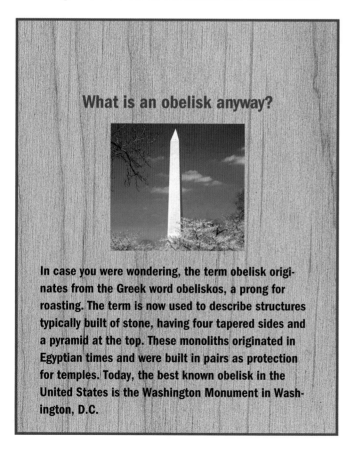

What is an obelisk anyway?

In case you were wondering, the term obelisk originates from the Greek word obeliskos, a prong for roasting. The term is now used to describe structures typically built of stone, having four tapered sides and a pyramid at the top. These monoliths originated in Egyptian times and were built in pairs as protection for temples. Today, the best known obelisk in the United States is the Washington Monument in Washington, D.C.

template, draw a line bisecting the back of the hole and continue that line around the sides of the guide. You'll use these lines to line up the guide on the legs. Drill ⅜-in.-deep pipe holes in each leg using a ⅝-in. Forstner bit **(Photo B).**

Cut the top and bottom crosspieces from the remaining 2×2 cedar **(Photo C).** I used a power miter saw to make these cuts, but you could lay out the cut lines with a protractor and cut the pieces with a handsaw.

At this point you can finish all the cedar parts, including the cap, with exterior stain sealer before assembly. This optional step helps maintain the color, balances any tonal differences between pieces and protects the wood from the elements. Be sure to mask off the crosspiece connection areas with tape to provide clean surfaces for glue penetration.

The final preparation step before assembly is to measure and cut the copper tubing. Clamp two adjacent legs and their corresponding top and bottom crosspieces together on a work surface. Determine the pipe lengths by measuring between the legs at each pipe level and adding ¾ in.

Before cutting the pipe, you'll want to remove the stamped information that appears on the tubing. You can use steel wool or a shop towel dipped in lacquer thinner. The lacquer thinner makes fast work of the ink. Be sure to wear neoprene gloves for protection.

You can cut copper pipe several ways. A miter saw equipped with a metal-cutting blade works well, especially when cutting multiple pieces of the same length. A hacksaw also works but is much more labor-intensive. I used a plumber's copper tubing cutter, which scores through the tubing. Start by placing it over the tubing and tighten the handle until the cutting wheel hits the cut line. Score through the copper by rotating the cutter around the pipe, tightening the cutting wheel after every couple of rotations **(Photo D).** The freshly cut ends will be sharp, so handle them with care.

ASSEMBLY

The basic approach to assembling the obelisk is to join two opposite sides individually and then connect them to form the structure. This part of the project requires patience. If you've ever worked on a project with spindles, such as a bench or chair, you can probably predict that sandwiching 11 pipes between two

A

Clamp all four legs together with one of the inside faces up. Measure and mark the pipe-hole locations using a pencil and combination square.

B

Drill the pipe holes using a shop-made drill guide. The drill bit is marked with a piece of tape to act as a depth guide.

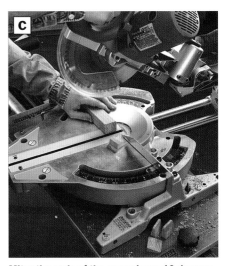

C

Miter the ends of the crosspieces 10 degrees.

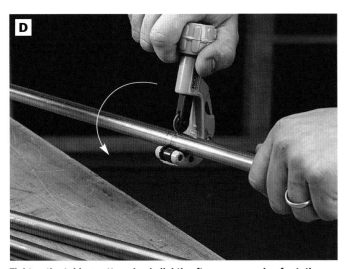

D

Tighten the tubing cutter wheel slightly after every couple of rotations.

E

Work the pipes into their holes starting at the bottom. The pipes "float" in place; no glue or fasteners are needed.

legs will be a challenge. The key, as with most assemblies, is to be calm and organized.

Remove the top clamp from the side assembly and pull the tops of the legs apart just enough to allow the bottom pipe into its holes. Now fit the next piece of pipe into its holes and pull the tops of the legs together just enough to barely hold it in position. Continue working up the legs until all the pipes are resting in their holes **(Photo E).** Next, dry-fit (without glue) the top crosspiece between the two legs and clamp it in place. Check the fit of all the pipes. There can be a little play in each pipe but not so much that you can work it out of its holes. If a pipe is too loose, first check to see whether one of the other pipes is not fully seated in its holes. If the other pipes seem to fit correctly, you will need to replace the loose pipe with a longer piece.

Ten great climbing plants

Cathedral bells (Rhodochiton atrosanguineum)
Clematis (Clematis species)
Climbing nasturtium (Tropaeolum majus)
Climbing snapdragon (Asarina antirrhiniflora)
Clockvine (Thunbergia alata)
Hyacinth bean (Dolichos lablab)
Mandevilla (Mandevilla species)
Passionflower (Passiflora sanguinolenta)
Scarlet runner bean (Phaseolus coccineus)
Sweet peas (Lathyrus odoratus)

After fitting all the pipes into position, apply polyurethane glue to the crosspieces and screw them in place with 2½-in. stainless steel screws.

Work the pipes for the final two sides in from top to bottom. Complete one side, secure the crosspieces, flip the piece over and complete the final side.

Drill pilot holes; then drive 1½-in. galvanized finish nails through the post cap into each leg.

When you are satisfied with the fit of all the pipes, back off the top clamp just enough to slip out the top crosspiece. Apply polyurethane glue to the ends of the top crosspiece. Insert the top crosspiece in place and retighten the clamp. Drill a pilot hole and then drive a 2½-in. stainless steel screw through one of the legs and the crosspiece and into the other leg (**Photo F**). Now back off the bottom clamp and repeat the gluing process with the bottom crosspiece. Once the screws are in you can remove the clamps and repeat the process to create the opposite side. Scrape off any dried foam left by the polyurethane glue with a chisel or knife.

Connecting the two side assemblies is easier with a helper. Rather than try to line up all the pipes for both remaining sides at once, I found it much easier to complete one side at a time.

Set the two side assemblies on their sides with the pipe holes facing each other. Screw and glue the top crosspiece in place — this helps stabilize the assembly. Fit the pipes into the holes just as you did on the individual sides, except this time work from top to bottom. When you are happy with the fit of all the pipes, glue and screw the bottom crosspiece in place. Now flip the project over and repeat the steps for the final side (**Photo G**).

Secure the post cap with 1½-in. galvanized finish nails driven through the sides of the cap into each leg (**Photo H**). Be sure to drill pilot holes for these nails first.

Before installing the garden obelisk in your yard, drive one No. 8 × 1⅝-in. screw eye into the bottom inside corner of each leg for stakes to run through.

INSTALLATION

Installing the garden obelisk is as simple as choosing a location and staking it in place. Then all that's left is to choose a plant and wait for it to start climbing. To help you get started, I enlisted the help of Justin Hancock, horticulture editor for *Gardening How-To,* a publication of the National Home Gardening Club. He prepared a list of 10 excellent climbing-plant candidates (see sidebar, p. 127). If you're not sure what type of plant will thrive in your region, consult a local nursery.

Dan Cary, *writer*
Mark Macemon, *photography*
Gabriel Graphics, *illustration*

Table to Go

I f you've ever had a barbecue, hosted a card game or planned a picnic, you've probably needed an extra table. The small folding tables available at most stores are serviceable, but they're typically rather ugly and require a tablecloth to cover the plastic or metal frame. As an attractive alternative, we designed a table that seats four and folds up for storage. But it looks so good that you won't want to put it away.

Table to Go

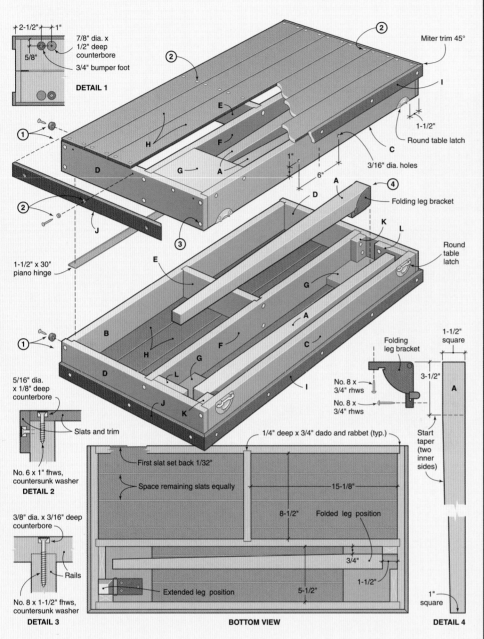

DETAIL 1

2-1/2" · 1"
5/8"
7/8" dia. x 1/2" deep counterbore
3/4" bumper foot

Miter trim 45°

1-1/2"
Round table latch

3/16" dia. holes

1"
6"

Folding leg bracket

Round table latch

1-1/2" x 30" piano hinge

5/16" dia. x 1/8" deep counterbore

Slats and trim

DETAIL 2
No. 6 x 1" fhws, countersunk washer

3/8" dia. x 3/16" deep counterbore

Rails

DETAIL 3
No. 8 x 1-1/2" fhws, countersunk washer

1/4" deep x 3/4" dado and rabbet (typ.)
First slat set back 1/32"
Space remaining slats equally
15-1/8"
8-1/2" Folded leg position
3/4"
1-1/2"
Extended leg position
5-1/2"

BOTTOM VIEW

Folding leg bracket
No. 8 x 3/4" rhws
No. 8 x 3/4" rhws

1-1/2" square
3-1/2"
Start taper (two inner sides)
1" square

DETAIL 4

Shopping List

- ☐ ¾ × 6 × 96-in. mahogany (3)
- ☐ 1½ × 1½ × 120-in. mahogany (1)
- ☐ Folding leg brackets, No. 00T16.01 (2 pairs)
- ☐ 1½ × 36-in. piano hinge (1)
- ☐ Round table latches, No. 00A51.04 (2)
- ☐ No. 6 countersunk washers, No. 01K70.01 (86)
- ☐ No. 8 countersunk washers, No. 01K70.02 (48)
- ☐ No. 6 × 1-in. brass screws (86)
- ☐ No. 8 × 1½-in. brass screws (48)
- ☐ No. 8 × 1¼-in. brass screws (12)
- ☐ No. 8 × ¾-in. panhead screws (24)
- ☐ ¾-in. bumper feet, No. 00S51.03 (4)
- ☐ ½-in.-dia. × 4-ft. white nylon rope
- ☐ Exterior-grade wood glue
- ☐ ⁵⁄₁₆-in. Forstner bit, No. 06J71.05
- ☐ ³⁄₈-in. Forstner bit, No. 06J71.06
- ☐ ⁷⁄₈-in. Forstner bit, No. 06J71.14

Materials and Cutting List

Part/Description	No.	Size	Part/Description	No.	Size
A Legs	4	1½ × 1½ × 28½ in.	G Leg cleats	4	¾ × 5½ × 5½ in.
B Inside rails	2	¾ × 2¹⁵⁄₁₆ × 31½ in.	H Top slats	12	⁵⁄₁₆ × 2⅝ × 32½ in.
C Front rails	2	¾ × 3 × 31½ in.	I Front trim rails	2	⁵⁄₁₆ × 1¼ × 33 in.
D Side rails	4	¾ × 3 × 16¼ in.	J Side trim rails	4	⁵⁄₁₆ × 1¼ × 16½ in.
E Cross rails	2	¾ × 2¹⁵⁄₁₆ × 9 in.	K Small leg brace	4	¾ × 1½ × 2¼ in.
F Middle rails	2	¾ × 3 × 31½ in.	L Large leg brace	4	¾ × 2¼ × 3¼ in.

Table to Go: Instructions

The table is the size of a card table and folds in half like a suitcase. It's made of mahogany with brass hardware and a rope handle. The materials give the table a nautical style that is further reflected in the tabletop slats, which are reminiscent of the decking on a classic wooden boat.

This project will put your whole shop to work, including your table saw, band saw, drill press and surface planer. In case you don't have all of the tools I used, I've included alternative methods for some of the techniques. Of course, you could use this project as an excuse to pick up a new tool or two.

ASSEMBLING THE TABLETOP FRAME

The rail pieces are 3 in. wide except for the inside and cross rails, which are $2^{15}/_{16}$ in. to create a recess

for the hinge. You'll need to rip surfaced $^3/_4$-in.-thick stock to the correct widths for the rail pieces and then cut them to length. Cross-cut $^1/_4$-in.-deep × $^3/_4$-in.-wide dadoes and rabbets in the side, middle and inside rails using a table saw or router.

I fastened all of the table frame joints with glue and brass screws. I used brass countersunk washers under all exposed screwheads (see "Countersunk Washers," p. 132), but they are not required — you can simply countersink the screws without washers.

Use a drill press equipped with a $^3/_8$-in.-dia. Forstner bit to bore the $^3/_{16}$-in.-deep counterbores for the washers (**Photo A**). A good alternative to a drill press is a portable drill guide attachment (available at most woodworking stores).

Attach the inside rail and middle rail to the cross rail first; then attach the side rails and front rail. Use a ratcheting screwdriver to help prevent stripping the slotted brass screws. Next, glue and clamp the leg cleats to the front rail, middle rail and side rail (**Photo B**).

MILLING SLATS AND TRIM RAILS

The top slats are thin ($^5/_{16}$ in.) to help reduce the overall weight of the table. You can mill the slats your-

A

$^3/_8$-in.-dia. Forstner bit

Bore $^3/_8$-in.-dia. × $^3/_{16}$-in.-deep counterbores for the No. 8 countersunk washers. Mark the position of the Forstner bit's center on a fence to position the rails.

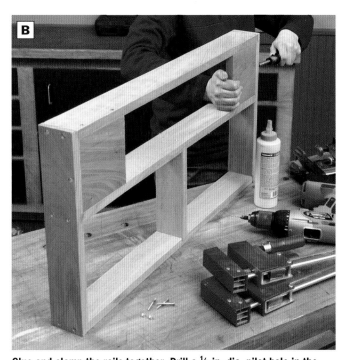

B

Glue and clamp the rails together. Drill a $^1/_8$-in.-dia. pilot hole in the center of each counterbore, and fasten each joint with a No. 8 × 1½-in. brass screw and countersunk washer.

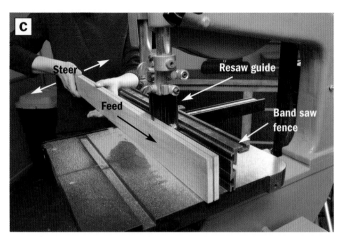

Resaw ¾-in.-thick stock in half to create the top slat and trim rail stock. Position the resaw guide so that the blade is centered on the workpiece. Move the back end of the workpiece, pivoting on the resaw guide, to guide the stock.

Attach the top slats and trim rails with No. 6 × 1-in. brass screws and countersunk washers. A ratcheting screwdriver works well for driving the slotted screws.

self, have them milled for you at a full-service lumberyard or substitute ½- or ¾-in.-thick stock, which is easier to find. If you substitute thicker stock, remember to add the extra thickness to the trim rail width.

To create the 5⁄16-in.-thick stock for the top and trim rails, I resawed ¾-in.-thick stock using a band saw. Resawing is simply cutting a board on edge to create thinner pieces, a technique commonly used to cut veneers. The key to successful resawing is using a blade that is appropriate and sharp. I used a ½-in.-wide hook-tooth blade with three teeth per inch.

Band saws often cut at a slight angle to the direction of feed, a characteristic known as "drift" or "lead." This means that you can't simply clamp a

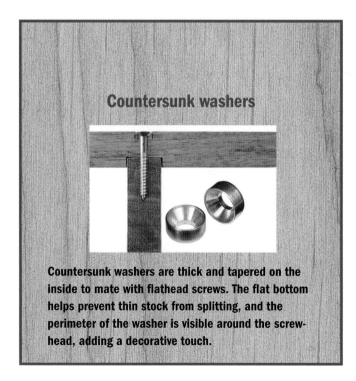

Countersunk washers

Countersunk washers are thick and tapered on the inside to mate with flathead screws. The flat bottom helps prevent thin stock from splitting, and the perimeter of the washer is visible around the screwhead, adding a decorative touch.

fence perpendicular to the front of the table and expect the saw to cut parallel to the fence. There are two ways to compensate for this problem. The first is to adjust the band saw fence to match the angle of blade lead. The second is to use a guide or single-pivot point known as a resaw guide. I used a manufactured resaw guide, but you can easily make one (see "Make a Resaw Guide," p. 133).

Cut seven boards to ¾ × 2⅝ × 34 in. and then draw a line down the center of one long edge of each board. Position the resaw guide so that the blade will track down the center of the line. Use the resaw guide as a pivot, steering each board through the cut by moving the tail or back of the board **(Photo C).** Move to the front of the board and pull the board through to finish the cut. If this is your first time resawing, practice cutting scrap pieces to get the hang of it.

After resawing all of the boards, run them through a thickness planer to remove the blade marks and bring them to the final thickness, which should be about ¼ to 5⁄16 in. Then cut the 12 top slats to final length and mark the screw positions on the top faces.

Rip the two remaining pieces of thin stock into 1-¼-in.-wide strips for the trim rails. Miter-cut two of the pieces to a final length of 33 in. Next, cut the four side trim rails to 16½ in. with miters on one end only (see "Bottom View" detail, p. 130).

Set up a drill press fence so that the bit centers ⅜ in. from the fence. Bore 5⁄16-in.-dia. × ⅛-in.-deep counterbores for No. 6 countersunk washers in the top slats and trim rails. Sand the faces and ease the edges of each piece; then attach them to the tabletop frame **(Photo D).** Once all of the pieces are secure, sand the surfaces and countersunk washers flush.

Build the taper jig. Align the leg taper layout marks on the edge of the plywood. Trace the leg profile on the plywood.

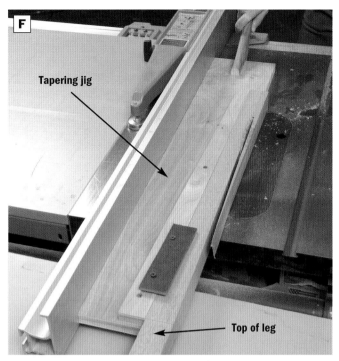

Position the leg in the taper jig and cut the first taper. Use a pushstick to guide the jig through the cut. Turn the leg one-quarter turn so that the first tapered side faces up, and cut the second taper.

MAKING THE TABLE LEGS

I tapered the legs using a table saw and a tapering jig. A tapering jig securely holds the leg blank at an angle as it is cut. If you plan to do more projects with tapered legs, consider buying an adjustable tapering jig. I chose to make a simple tapering jig for this project. It requires a small flat scrap of plywood and takes only a few minutes.

To make the jig, first mark the end points of the taper on one of the leg blanks. Measure down $3\frac{1}{2}$ in. from the top on the side of the leg, and measure in $\frac{1}{2}$ in. from the same side on the bottom. Position the leg blank on top of a $\frac{3}{4} \times 6 \times 30$-in. piece of plywood so that the two lines intersect the left edge of the plywood. Trace the outline of the leg blank on the plywood **(Photo E).** Next, cut along the traced lines, removing the portion of the plywood that was overlapped by the leg blank. Attach the cutoff piece flush with the long cut edge of the main plywood jig. Finally, attach a small scrap near the front of the jig to act as a hold-down.

Position the table saw fence so its distance from the blade matches the width of the tapering jig. Put the leg blank into the jig and make the first taper cut, using a pushstick for safety. Taper one side of the leg **(Photo F);** then turn the leg to taper one of the adjacent sides. Scrape or sand away the blade marks when you're done.

FASTENING THE HARDWARE

Before attaching the hardware, sand and apply the finish of your choice (I used a wipe-on oil) to the tabletop and legs. For the folding mechanism, I bought a $1\frac{1}{2}$- × 36-in. piano hinge (available at most home centers) and cut it to 30 in. long with a hacksaw.

Make a resaw guide

Pivot block

Pivot block

A resaw guide is simply a pivot block that acts as a fence, establishing the thickness of the resaw cut. To make one, all you need is a 5-in.-long scrap of 2×6 lumber. Taper the leading edges of the stock and cut away some of the back edge, leaving a clamping surface for securing the guide to the band saw table.

Place the two tabletop halves facedown on a flat surface with the inside rails butted together. Fasten the piano hinge to both rails with $\frac{3}{4}$-in. flathead brass screws.

Next, fasten one folding leg bracket to each leg

Fasten the legs and leg brackets with the tapered sides facing toward the inside. Then fasten the brackets to the leg cleats. The legs should fit snugly between the leg braces.

³⁄₈-in.-deep x ⁷⁄₈-in.-dia. counter bore

Offset the four rubber feet and counterbores so that when the table is opened each foot will fit into a counterbored recess. Use a ⁷⁄₈-in.-dia. Forstner bit to bore the recesses.

with No. 8 × ³⁄₄-in. panhead screws. Fasten the small and large leg braces to the front and side rails using No. 8 × 1¼-in. screws. Then fasten the folding leg brackets to the leg cleats using No. 8 × ³⁄₄-in. panhead screws (**Photo G**).

Two 2¼-in. round brass table latches hold the table closed. These table latches are normally concealed underneath a tabletop and used to hold table leaves together, but they also work for this application, and I like the decorative appearance. Close the tabletop and fasten the front latches.

Attach four rubber feet to the inside rail, and drill ⁷⁄₈-in.-dia. × ½-in.-deep counterbores for the feet to fit into when the table opens (**Photo H and detail 1 in the illustration**).

The final step is to attach the rope handles. Tie two knots 8 in. apart in two 20-in.-long pieces of ½-in. braided nylon rope. Trim the loose ends to 1 in. long. Singe each end with a match or lighter to keep it from fraying. Next, drill two ³⁄₁₆-in.-dia. holes 6 in. apart in each front rail. Feed mason's line through each hole from the inside of the rail, wrap the line around the rope and then feed the line back through the hole. Repeat this process to create two loops over the rope. Snug the loops of mason's line down next to the knots (**Photo I**) and tie the loose ends of the line

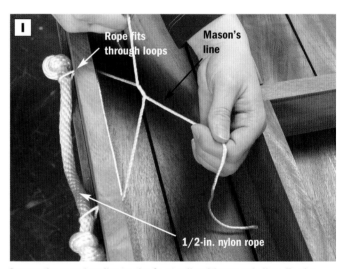

Rope fits through loops — Mason's line

1/2-in. nylon rope

Secure the rope handles to the front rails with mason's line. Feed a loop of the mason's line through each hole and then fit the rope handle through the loops. Snug the loops and tie the line tightly. Singe the ends of the line to prevent fraying.

together inside the front rail. The table is ready for entertaining, so start making plans.

Dan Cary, *writer*
Dan Cary, *photography*
Gabriel Graphics, *illustration*

Sports Caddy

Most of us encourage our children to play sports, but no one wants to come home to a garage that looks like a sporting goods store exploded. Providing a well-designed system for kids to store their stuff can make all the difference. And including your children or grandchildren in the construction process can foster a sense of ownership in the project and help ensure they'll actually use it.

Sports Caddy

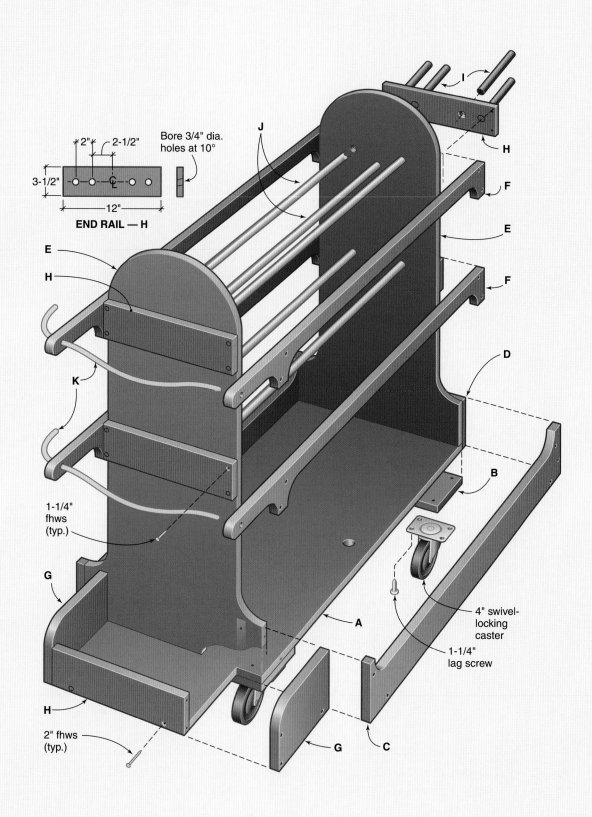

2"

2-1/2"

3-1/2"

C

12"

END RAIL — H

Bore 3/4" dia.
holes at 10°

J

E

H

I

H

F

E

F

D

K

B

1-1/4"
fhws
(typ.)

4" swivel-
locking
caster

1-1/4"
lag screw

G

A

H

G

C

2" fhws
(typ.)

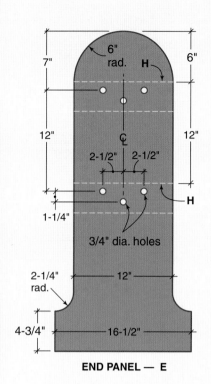

END PANEL — E

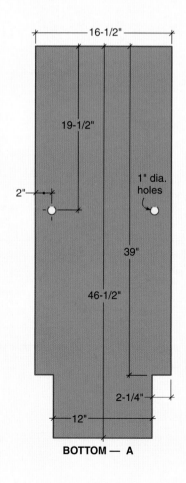

BOTTOM — A

Hardware			
Part/Description		**No.**	**Size**
A	Bottom, plywood	1	$\frac{3}{4} \times 16\frac{1}{2} \times 46\frac{1}{2}$ in.
B	Caster cleats, pine	2	$\frac{3}{4} \times 5\frac{1}{2} \times 16\frac{1}{2}$ in.
C	Bottom rails, pine	2	$\frac{3}{4} \times 5\frac{1}{2} \times 39\frac{3}{4}$ in.
D	Bottom end rail, pine	1	$\frac{3}{4} \times 5\frac{1}{2} \times 16\frac{1}{2}$ in.
E	End panels, plywood	2	$\frac{3}{4} \times 16\frac{1}{2} \times 38$ in.
F	Side rails, pine	4	$\frac{3}{4} \times 3\frac{1}{2} \times 48$ in.
G	Box side rails, pine	2	$\frac{3}{4} \times 5\frac{1}{2} \times 8\frac{1}{4}$ in.
H	End rails, pine	5	$\frac{3}{4} \times 3\frac{1}{2} \times 12$ in.
I	Dowels, oak	4	$\frac{3}{4} \times 8$ in.
J	Ball tracks, EMT conduit	6	$\frac{3}{4} \times 39$ in.
K	Rope ends, nylon rope	2	$\frac{1}{2} \times 18$ in.

Shopping List

- ☐ $\frac{3}{4} \times 24 \times 48$-in. plywood (3)
- ☐ 1×4 × 8-ft. pine (3)
- ☐ 1×6 × 8-ft. pine (2)
- ☐ $\frac{3}{4}$-in.-dia. × 10-ft. EMT conduit (2)
- ☐ 4-in. swivel-locking casters (4)
- ☐ $\frac{3}{4}$-in.-dia. × 36-in. wood dowel (1)
- ☐ $1\frac{1}{4}$-in. exterior-grade screws
- ☐ 2-in. exterior-grade screws
- ☐ $\frac{1}{4} \times 1\frac{1}{2}$-in. galvanized lag screws
- ☐ Exterior primer (1 quart)
- ☐ Exterior acrylic paint
- ☐ $\frac{1}{2}$-in. nylon rope (4 ft.)

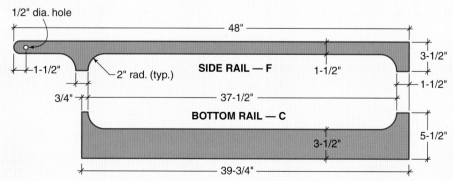

SIDE RAIL — F

BOTTOM RAIL — C

Sports Caddy: Instructions

With these goals in mind I designed a cart that holds a lot of gear, looks good, doesn't take up much space and rolls wherever it's needed. It features two rails that each hold four full-size basketballs or a variety of smaller balls such as soccer balls, a large bottom shelf for everything from in-line skates to baseball gloves, a vertical storage area for long items such as bats or hockey sticks and a rack for hanging skateboards and helmets.

This design is also easy to modify to suit other storage needs. For example, removing the ball tracks and securing a couple of $\frac{3}{4} \times 14\frac{1}{2} \times 36$-in. plywood shelves on the side rails makes the cart perfect for storing power tool cases, gardening materials or automotive supplies.

CUTTING THE PARTS

When shopping for materials, I bought 2 × 4-ft. birch plywood panels, which are a little more expensive but easier to haul and handle than full-size sheets. Cut all of the plywood and solid stock parts to the dimensions in the cutting list; then refer to the drawing (p. 137) to lay out the profiles on the bottom, one end panel, two side rails and one bottom rail **(Photo A)**. Next, clamp matching parts together and cut them in pairs with a jigsaw **(Photo B)**.

The ball tracks fit through holes in the end panels and are held in place by the end rails. Mark the center location of each rail and drill a 1-in.-dia. hole at each mark.

Drill two 1-in.-dia. drain holes in the bottom. I located the holes 2 in. from the side rails and centered them between the end panels, but the spacing is not critical.

To make the dowel rack, fasten four dowels to one of the end rails. Drill four $\frac{3}{4}$-in.-dia. holes at a 10-degree angle through one of the end rails **(Photo C)**. Next, cut four 8-in.-long pieces of $\frac{3}{4}$-in.-dia. dowel and secure them to the end rail holes with exterior-grade glue.

Sand all of the parts smooth. Apply one coat of exterior-grade primer and two coats of exterior-grade paint to all surfaces. I chose a basic two-color paint scheme, but you can be as creative as you like with the color choices. You might also want to personalize the cart by painting images of your child's favorite sports or your child's name — ask for his or her input.

ASSEMBLING THE CART

When assembling the parts, you'll work up from

A

End panel

Bottom rail

Use a compass, combination square and straightedge to draw the profiles on all of the shaped parts and to mark all of the hole locations (see drawing, p. 137).

B

Cut along the layout lines with a jigsaw. Cut the parts in pairs to save time and achieve more consistent results.

Drill four angled dowel holes in one of the end rails. Use a portable drill guide, or cut a 10-degree miter in a scrap of 1×4 to act as an angle guide for the drill. Use a scrap piece as a backer block to prevent splintering.

Attach the end panels to the bottom with 2-in. deck screws. Then attach the caster cleats with 1¼-in. deck screws.

Slide the pieces of EMT conduit through the holes in the end panels and secure them in place by attaching the end rails with 1¼-in. screws.

Fasten the casters to the caster cleats with ¼ × 1½-in. lag screws and washers. Drill a ³⁄₁₆-in.-dia. pilot hole for each bolt.

the bottom using exterior-rated screws. To avoid splitting the stock, drill countersunk pilot holes and be careful not to overtighten the screws.

First, attach the end panels to the bottom with 2-in. screws, being careful to keep the end panels perpendicular to the bottom **(Photo D).** Then attach the caster cleats to the bottom with 1¼-in. screws. Next, attach the bottom rails, the side rails and the box side rails.

I used ¾-in.-dia. electrical metal tubing (EMT) conduit for the ball tracks. Use a hacksaw to cut six 39-in.-long pieces of the conduit. Slide the conduit through the holes in the vertical panels. Then cover the conduit ends by attaching the end rails to the vertical panels with 1¼-in. screws **(Photo E)** and fasten the side rails to the end rails with 2-in. screws.

I used nylon rope for the end rails on the tall vertical storage area. Slide the rope through the holes in the side rails, tie knots in the ends and trim off any excess. To keep the ends from fraying, singe them with a match or lighter.

Finally, fasten the casters to the caster cleats with four ¼ × 1½-in. lag screws and washers **(Photo F).** The cart is now ready for service. It won't clean up a messy garage on its own, but it might increase the odds that someone else will.

Dan Cary, *writer and photography*
Gabriel Graphics, *illustration*

Chapter 3

Shop

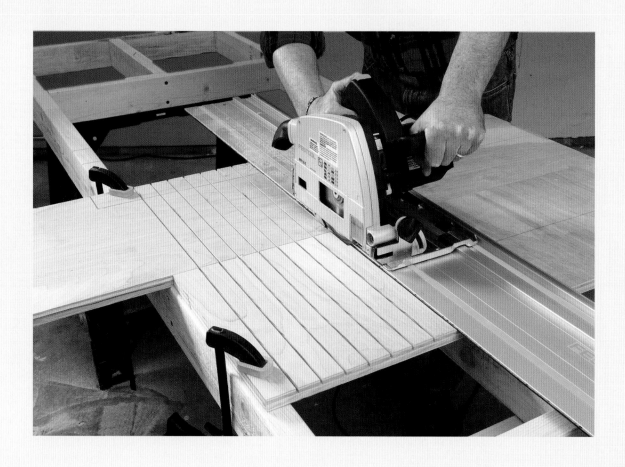

Small-Shop Solution

However you've organized your shop space, there's a good chance that you store some tools on perfboard. The stuff's been around for ages, but it's still one of the most economical ways to keep frequently used tools organized, in plain view and easily accessible. Perfboard hooks come in a wide variety of shapes and sizes, so you can hang just about any kind of tool. But perfboard can eat up a lot of wall space, and if your shop is small, you may be left with tools in need of a home. Here's a solution.

Small-Shop Solution

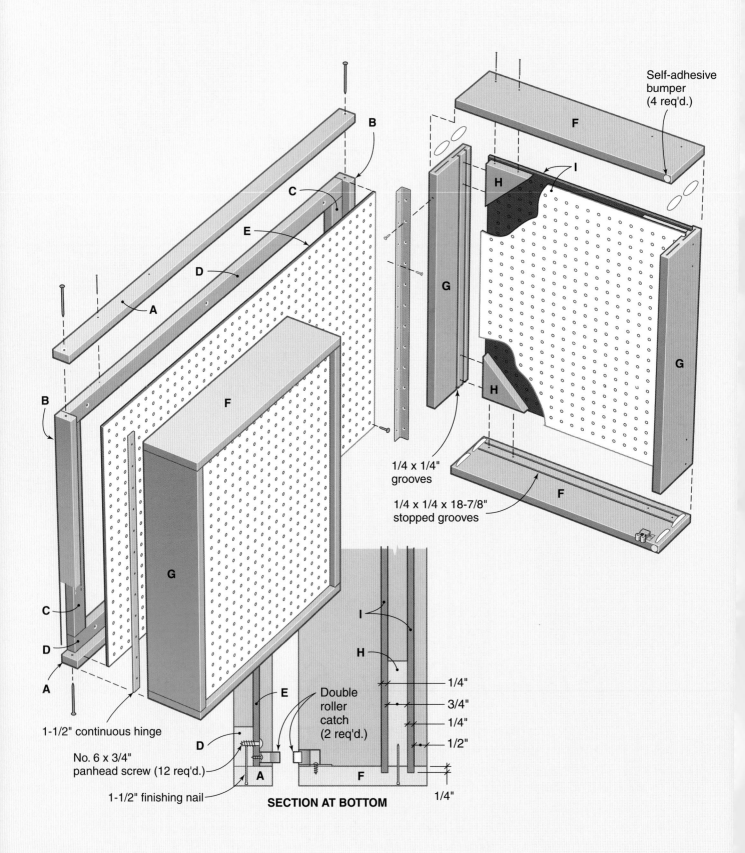

Self-adhesive bumper (4 req'd.)

F

H

I

G

G

B

C

E

D

A

B

C

D

A

F

G

F

1/4 x 1/4" grooves

1/4 x 1/4 x 18-7/8" stopped grooves

I

H

1/4"

3/4"

1/4"

1/2"

1-1/2" continuous hinge

No. 6 x 3/4" panhead screw (12 req'd.)

1-1/2" finishing nail

D

E

A

Double roller catch (2 req'd.)

F

SECTION AT BOTTOM

1/4"

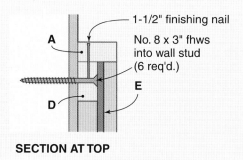

1-1/2" finishing nail

No. 8 x 3" fhws
into wall stud
(6 req'd.)

A

D

E

SECTION AT TOP

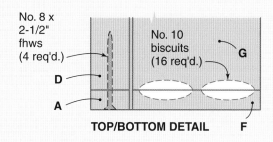

No. 8 x
2-1/2"
fhws
(4 req'd.)

D

A

No. 10
biscuits
(16 req'd.)

G

F

TOP/BOTTOM DETAIL

Shopping List

- [ ] 48 × 96-in. coated perf-board (1)
- [ ] ¾ × 1½ × 108-in. poplar (3)
- [ ] ¾ × 5½ × 120-in. poplar (2)
- [ ] No. 10 plate-joining biscuits (16)
- [ ] No. 8 × 2½-in. fhws (4)
- [ ] No. 8 × 3-in. fhws (6)
- [ ] 1½-in. nails for brad nailer
- [ ] No. 6 × 3-in. panhead screws (12)
- [ ] 1½ × 30-in. continuous hinge (2)
- [ ] Double-roller catches (2)
- [ ] Door bumpers (4)
- [ ] Yellow glue

Back Frame Cutting List

Part/Description		No.	Size
A	Top/bottom	2	¾ × 1½ × 40 in.
B	Sides	2	¾ × 1½ × 22½ in.
C	Side cleats	2	¾ × 1½ × 19½ in.
D	Top/bottom cleats	2	¾ × 1½ × 38½ in.
E	Perfboard face	1	¼ × 22½ × 38½ in.

Doors Cutting List

F	Tops/bottoms	4	¾ × 5 × 19⅞ in.
G	Sides	4	¾ × 5 × 22½ in.
H	Corner braces	8	¾ × 4 × 4 in.
I	Perfboard fronts/backs	4	¼ × 18⅞ × 23 in.

A shallow perfboard cabinet is the perfect solution for limited wall space. I made this cabinet to fit on the only remaining empty wall in my shop, which happened to be over a wood lathe. With the cabinet doors closed, the turning tools are right where I need them when I use the lathe. With the doors open, I have access to woodworking and mechanic's tools that I use at the bench opposite the lathe. But what's most important is that I gained three times the tool storage space with a cabinet that protrudes only 6½ in. from the wall.

Each cabinet door incorporates two perfboard panels (see drawing) with enough space between them so the back-frame hooks don't collide with those inside the doors. Continuous hinges provide sag-free support for the doors, even when they're fully loaded with tools. The distance between the perfboard on the back frame and the inside of the door (4 in. when closed) easily accommodates all but the widest tools.

Countless variations can be made to this basic design. By altering the dimensions of the parts, you can modify it to suit your available wall space and the tools you intend to store.

MATERIALS AND FRAME

This cabinet's construction is simple; it's made using butt joints fastened with glue, nails, screws and biscuits. All of the materials are available at any home center. I purchased lengths of milled 1½-in. and 5½-in. poplar (see Shopping List) and ripped the 5½-in. boards to 5 in.

Rather than using common tan perfboard, I opted for the slightly more expensive white-coated material. I prefer the white because it looks better and helps to keep the shop bright. (You can buy half sheets of perfboard, which are easier to transport.)

Begin by cutting all the parts to size and marking them to prevent confusion when you do the assembly. If you want the perfboard holes to be evenly spaced and aligned on the doors, you may need to trim the factory edges before you cut the pieces to size.

Assemble the back frame first. Glue and nail the top, bottom and sides together. Then drive No. 8 × 2½-in. flathead wood screws into the corners (**Photo A,** drawing, top/bottom detail). Next, glue and nail the top/bottom cleats and then the side cleats to the frame (**Photo B**). It's very important that the frame be square to ensure the doors hang straight. If the diagonal frame measurements are equal, the frame is square (**Photo C**).

A

Glue and nail the back frame members. Then drive No. 8 × 2½-in. wood screws into the corners.

B

Fasten the top/bottom cleats with glue and brads. Keep the assembly flat on the workbench to prevent twisting.

C

The back frame must be perfectly square. If the diagonal measurements are equal, the frame is square.

Cut the stopped grooves in the door tops and bottoms with a router table. Carefully lower the work onto the bit.

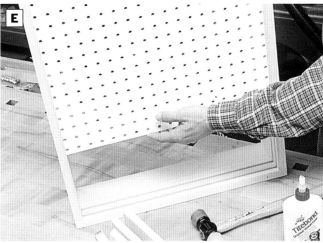

Assemble the sides and bottom; then slide the outside perfboard panel into its groove.

Next, glue and nail all four corner braces. Then glue the inside perfboard panel in position.

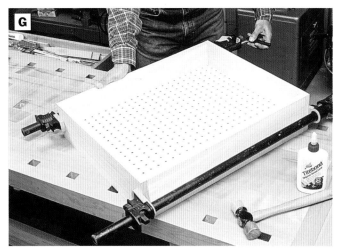

Install the top with biscuits and glue, then draw the joints tight with bar clamps. Check that the assembly is square.

DOOR CONSTRUCTION

Cut the grooves for the perfboard panels using a router table and ¼-in. straight bit or end mill (**Photo D**). The grooves on the top and bottom pieces should be stopped so they don't show on the ends. (This is purely an aesthetic consideration — you can cut the grooves with a table saw if you don't have a router table or a plunge router to cut stopped grooves.)

I used biscuits to join the door frame, but screws or dowels would work as well. The corner braces provide critical reinforcement in the corners to help prevent the doors from racking under load. These pieces must be cut perfectly square or they can force the door out of square when installed.

First assemble the sides and the bottom. Then slide the front panel into its groove (**Photo E**). Glue and nail all four corner braces into position. Be sure that the two top braces are flush with the top edges of the sides. Slide the inside panel into its groove along

with some glue (**Photo F**). Add the top and clamp the assembly (**Photo G**).

You may not be able to find 24-in. hinges, so you'll probably need to cut the hinges to the right length. Use a hacksaw and cut the hinges at the closest knuckle under 24 in.

You'll need to work methodically to install the hinges. Register a hinge leaf against the inside edge of the back frame side. Then, using a self-centering bit, bore three pilot holes at the top, bottom and middle of the hinge (**Photo H**). Install screws in these holes, then butt the doors against the frame and bore pilot holes for the opposing leaf hinge (**Photo I**). Install the screws and close the doors to check alignment. The doors should be flush with the sides of the back frame and have a ¼-in. gap between them. If the alignment is off, you'll need to cheat the position of the hinge leaf slightly. Bore the rest of the pilot holes and install all the screws in the frame-side hinge leaf.

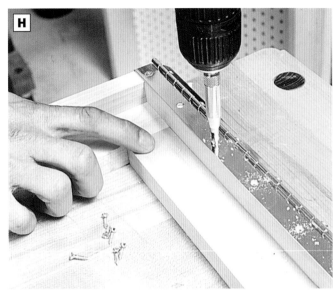

To ensure the continuous hinge is straight and doesn't bind, use a self-centering bit to bore the screw holes.

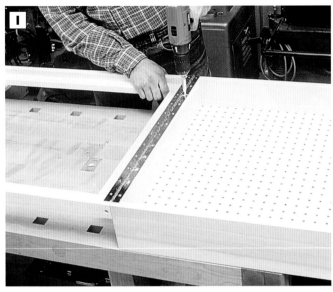

Screw the hinges to the back frame. Then butt the doors against the frame and fasten the hinges to the doors.

Find the wall studs and mark them. Screw through the back frame cleats into the studs with 3-in. screws.

Screw the perfboard panel to the back frame cleats with ¾-in. panhead screws.

Remove the screws on the door side of the hinge before mounting the cabinet on the wall. Locate the wall studs (you'll span three with this cabinet) and use a level as a guide to mark the centers with a pencil. Also, draw a horizontal line to mark the top of the cabinet, and indicate the ends with tick marks. If you install the cabinet near a corner, be sure there's enough clearance to allow the door to open completely without hitting the adjacent wall. Mount the frame with No. 8 × 3-in. flathead wood screws **(Photo J)**. (Drywall screws are brittle and can snap under a load.)

I left the perfboard panel off until after installing the back frame to make it easier to see and mark the stud centerlines. The panel also hides the mounting screws. To mount the panel, use about a dozen pan-head screws and drive them through the perfboard holes into the back frame cleats **(Photo K)**.

Enlist the help of a friend to install the doors. Mounting them can be tricky unless you can prop them so they're straight and stable. Once the doors are mounted, install the double-roller catches and door bumpers. You'll find these at any hardware store.

Larry Okrend, *writer*
Staff photos
Gabriel Graphics, *illustration*

Handy Workstation

The next time a light switch goes out or a pipe springs a leak in the middle of the night, don't waste valuable time searching for the necessary tools and supplies. The best way to avoid such hassles is to keep everything organized in one central location. This cabinet provides a perfect solution: It features an open work surface and a variety of storage options, such as lower cubbies sized to hold several tool cases.

Handy Workstation

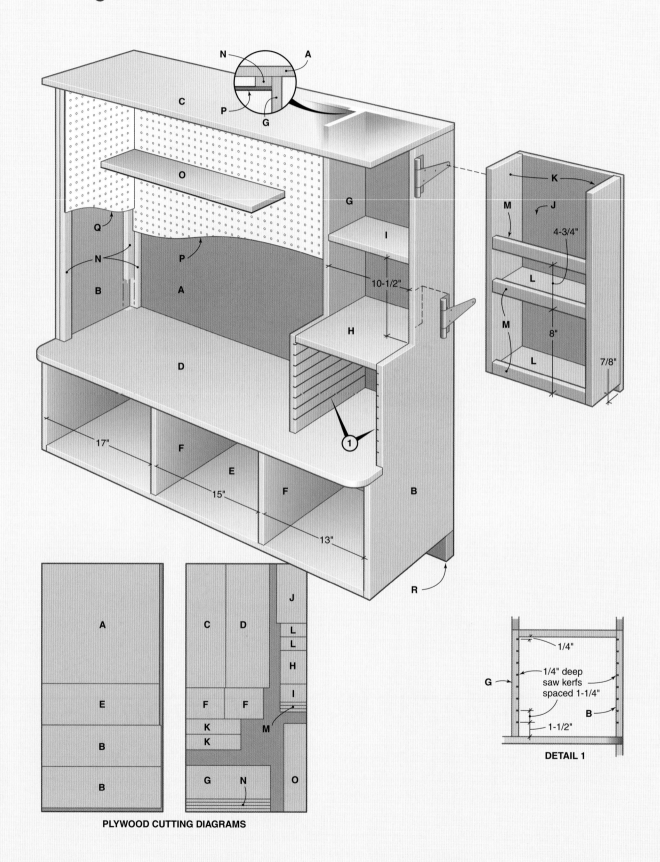

PLYWOOD CUTTING DIAGRAMS

DETAIL 1

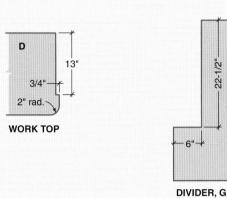

WORK TOP

D

13"

3/4"

2" rad.

DIVIDER, G

22-1/2"

6"

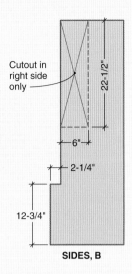

Cutout in
right side
only

22-1/2"

6"

2-1/4"

12-3/4"

SIDES, B

Shopping List

- [ ] ³/₄-in. × 4×8-ft. birch plywood (2)
- [ ] ¹/₄-in. × 4×8-ft. pegboard (1)
- [ ] 48-in. × 2×4 pine (framing stock)
- [ ] 1-in. toolbox tray
- [ ] 2-in. toolbox tray (2)
- [ ] 3-in. toolbox tray
- [ ] 4-in. T-hinges (2)
- [ ] ¹/₄ × 1¹/₄-in. machine screws (12)
- [ ] ¹/₄-in. washers
- [ ] ¹/₄-in. locknuts
- [ ] 2-in. coarse-thread screws
- [ ] 1¹/₄-in. coarse-thread screws
- [ ] ¹/₄ × 3-in. lag screws (6)
- [ ] ¹/₄-in. washers (6)
- [ ] Exterior satin or semigloss paint
- [ ] Pegboard hooks
- [ ] Power strip
- [ ] Suface-mount light fixture

³/₄-in. Birch Plywood Cutting List

Part/Description		No.	Size
A	Back	1	$\frac{3}{4} \times 46\frac{1}{2} \times 46\frac{1}{2}$ in.
B	Sides	2	$\frac{3}{4} \times 16 \times 47\frac{1}{4}$ in.
C	Top	1	$\frac{3}{4} \times 16 \times 48$ in.
D	Work top	1	$\frac{3}{4} \times 17\frac{1}{4} \times 48$ in.
E	Bottom	1	$\frac{3}{4} \times 16 \times 46\frac{1}{2}$ in.
F	Cubby dividers	2	$\frac{3}{4} \times 12 \times 15\frac{1}{4}$ in.
G	Vertical divider	1	$\frac{3}{4} \times 13 \times 33\frac{3}{4}$ in.
H	Bottom shelf	1	$\frac{3}{4} \times 10\frac{1}{2} \times 13$ in.
I	Upper shelf	1	$\frac{3}{4} \times 7 \times 10\frac{1}{2}$ in.
J	Door back	1	$\frac{3}{4} \times 12 \times 22\frac{7}{8}$ in.
K	Door sides	2	$\frac{3}{4} \times 6 \times 22$ in.
L	Door shelves	2	$\frac{3}{4} \times 5\frac{1}{4} \times 10\frac{1}{2}$ in.
M	Door shelf lips	3	$\frac{3}{4} \times 1\frac{1}{4} \times 10\frac{1}{2}$ in.
N	Pegboard spacers	4	$\frac{3}{4} \times 1\frac{1}{4} \times 33\frac{3}{4}$ in.
O	Adjustable shelf (opt.)	1	$\frac{3}{4} \times 5\frac{7}{8} \times 24$ in.

¹/₄-in. Pegboard Cutting List

P	Back pegboard	1	$\frac{1}{4} \times 33\frac{3}{4} \times 34\frac{1}{2}$ in.
Q	Side pegboard	1	$\frac{1}{4} \times 12 \times 33\frac{3}{4}$ in.

2×4 Pine Cutting List

R	Wall cleat	1	$1\frac{1}{2} \times 3\frac{1}{2} \times 48$ in.

A

Workpiece

2×4 frame

Use a circular saw or table saw to cut the plywood parts to size. Tip: Make a 2×4 frame to support the plywood during cutting. The size of the cutting frame is not critical; the frame shown is 27 in. × 78 in.

This project is intended to suit the storage needs of a homeowner with a basic set of hand tools and portable power tools, but it will also work well for specific purposes in an established shop. For example, it's an ideal sharpening center for storing chisels, planes and scrapers.

I included metal drawers and an overhead light in my design, but you can easily add any accessories you like, such as a small vise or large hooks on the sides for extension cords.

The cabinet carcase is built entirely of plywood, and you only need a circular saw, a jigsaw and a drill/driver to complete construction. The project costs less than $200, including the light, four metal drawers, a power strip and paint.

CUT THE PARTS

You'll need to set up a work surface for cutting the large sheets of plywood. The surface can be as simple as a couple of straight 2×4s placed on the garage floor, but it is safer and easier if you raise the surface to a comfortable working height. I like to place a simple 2×4 wood frame on a set of sawhorses.

You can buy a straightedge to guide your circular saw, or you can make your own. I used a straightedge and circular saw that are designed to work together to produce very accurate results (**Photo A**). For a fraction of the cost, you can also get great results from a shop-made straightedge (see "Circular Saw Straightedge," p. 152).

Follow the plywood cutting diagrams on p. 148 to make efficient use of your plywood. It's OK to mark a rough layout of the parts on the plywood for organizational purposes, but do not use these lines as cutting guides. This technique does not take into account the thickness of the blade kerf, so many of the pieces would be too small. For the most accurate results, measure and mark one cut at a time.

Mark the locations of the slots that will accept the

metal drawer trays on the right side and the vertical divider. The trays are designed to fit into slots the thickness of a saw blade kerf, about $\frac{1}{8}$ in. The slots are spaced $1\frac{1}{4}$ in. apart, allowing you to arrange the 1-, 2- and 3-in. drawer trays in different configurations to suit your needs. Set the circular saw to a cutting depth of $\frac{1}{4}$ in., and use a straightedge guide when cutting each slot (**Photo B**). Finally, cut the sides, vertical divider and work top to size with a jigsaw.

PAINT THE PARTS

Paint all of the parts before assembling the cabinet. Don't worry that the paint will interfere with glued joints — screws are the only fasteners necessary.

Sand all sides and edges of the parts with 150-grit sandpaper. Then apply one coat of primer and two coats of latex satin or semigloss paint to all plywood parts as well as the pegboard spacers and wall cleat. I used gray paint for all of the parts except the underside of the top and the left face of the vertical divider, which I painted white to match the pegboard. Use a roller or sprayer for the easiest application and smoothest finish.

Cut the ¼-in.-deep slots for the metal drawer trays in the right side and vertical divider at the same time. Space the slots 1¼ in. apart.

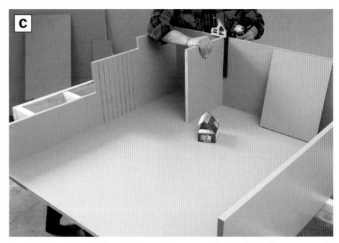

Attach the cubby dividers, sides and bottom to the back. Drill countersunk pilot holes and then secure each piece with 2-in. coarse-thread screws.

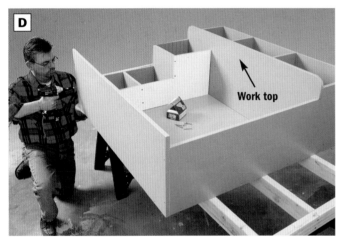

After attaching the work top, attach the vertical divider, shelves and top.

ASSEMBLE THE CABINET

Assemble the parts with 2-in. coarse-thread screws. (Drywall or deck screws work well.) Drill a countersink and pilot hole sized for a No. 8 screw before driving each screw.

Begin by attaching the sides, bottom and cubby dividers to the back (**Photo C**). Next, attach the work top and then the shelves and the vertical divider. Finally, attach the top (**Photo D**).

The door contains four fixed shelves. You can add, remove or reposition the shelves to suit your storage needs. Attach a shelf lip to each shelf; then attach the shelves to the door sides and door back. Attach one additional shelf lip 3½ in. above the top shelf lip.

HANG THE CABINET

You can hang the cabinet on a finished wall surface or on exposed studs. If the wall is finished, mark the stud locations. The cabinet must be fastened to at least two studs, so avoid aligning the sides over any studs. Place the cabinet on the floor in front of the studs.

Drill ¼-in. clearance holes through the back of the cabinet. Position the holes in line with the stud markings.

Mark the stud locations on the cabinet; then measure down 3 in. and 24 in. from the top. Drill ¼-in.-dia. clearance holes through the cabinet back (**Photo E**).

I positioned the wall cleat 28 in. above the floor and anchored it to the studs with 3-in. screws. At this mounting height the work top ends up 42 in. above the floor and there is room under the cabinet for a shop vacuum. With a helper, lift the cabinet onto the cleat. Using the clearance holes as a guide, drill ³⁄₁₆-in.-dia. pilot holes in the studs. Attach the cabinet to the wall with ¼ × 3-in. lag screws (**Photo F**).

Mark the hinge-hole locations on the side of the

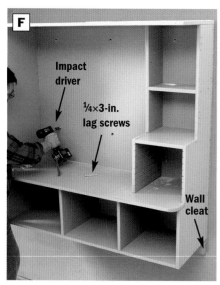

Lift the cabinet onto the wall cleat with a helper. Drill ³⁄₁₆-in. pilot holes in the studs at each clearance hole location; then drive lag screws into the studs.

Fasten the hinges to the door first; then attach the hinges to the cabinet. Use a piece of cardboard as a spacer under the door.

Attach the pegboard spacers and pegboard to the left side and back of the cabinet.

Circular saw straightedge

This straightedge guide is easy to build — it has only two parts. The first is a base piece made from ¼-in.-thick plywood or hardboard that is 12 in. wide and as long as 8 ft. The second is an edge guide made from a straight ¾-in.-thick × 2-in.-wide piece of solid wood or plywood that is the same length as the base piece.

Offset the edge guide on the base piece, leaving enough material on one side of the edge guide for the full width of the saw's baseplate. Drill countersinks in the base piece; then drive ¾-in. wood screws through the base and into the edge guide.

Next, trim the base piece by running the saw along the edge guide. The trimmed edge of the base piece now matches the saw's cutting line, and the jig is ready to use. Simply align the trimmed edge of the jig with the cutting line on the workpiece, clamp the jig in place and make the cut.

door. Drill ¼-in.-dia. pilot holes at each location. Fasten the hinges to the door with ¼- × 1¼-in. machine screws and locknuts. Then place a ⅛-in.-thick spacer under the door (a piece of corrugated cardboard works well) and position the door flush with the right cabinet side. Drill pilot holes and fasten the hinges to the cabinet side (**Photo G**).

Now install the pegboard, power strip and lighting. The pegboard must be spaced away from the cabinet back and sides to provide room for the hooks. Attach the pegboard spacer strips with 1¼-in. screws. Then fasten the pegboard to the spacers with 1¼-in. screws (**Photo H**).

Fasten the power strip to the bottom right corner of the pegboard. Drill 1¼-in. exit holes for the cord through the work top and bottom.

Next, follow the manufacturer's instructions for installing the lights. I chose to use an 18-in. fluorescent fixture. You could also use a set of under-cabinet halogen "puck" or pot lights.

I included an additional shelf that hangs on the pegboard. The adjustable shelf is supported by brackets that hang on the pegboard (available where pegboard hooks are sold).

Finally, install the metal drawer trays and fill the cabinet with your tools and supplies. The next time you need to repair something, you'll know where to find the right tool for the job.

Dan Cary, *writer*
Mark Macemon, *photography*
Gabriel Graphics, *illustration*

Robust Bench

Awoodworker's bench isn't just a work surface; it's a tool — maybe the hardest-working tool in any shop. Hardwood construction and elaborate joinery typically make these benches expensive, but you can build a lower-cost bench that works just as well as high-priced versions.

Robust Bench

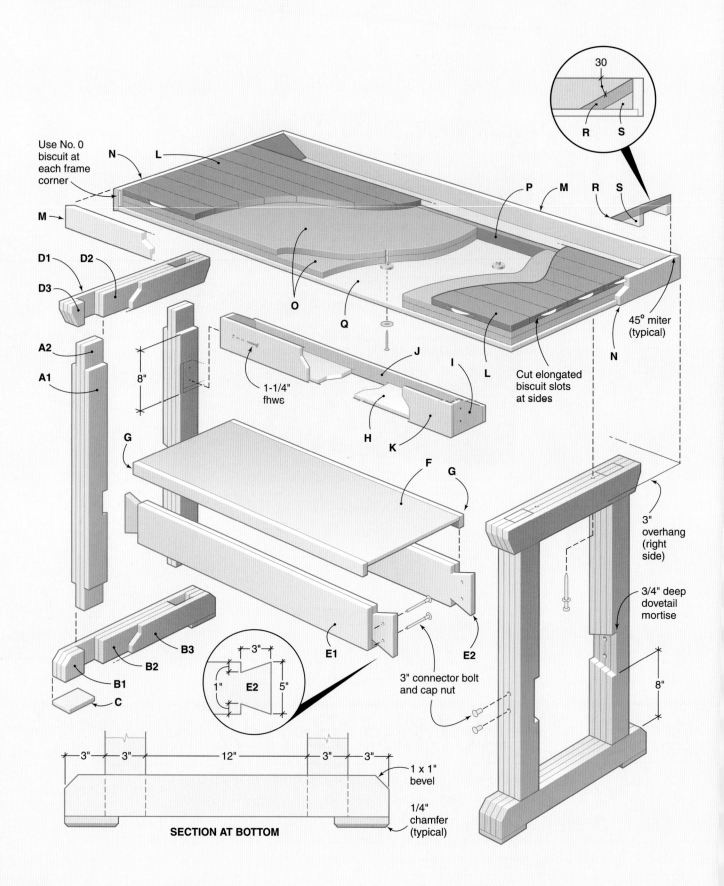

Use No. 0 biscuit at each frame corner

N   L

30

R   S

M

P   M   R   S

D1   D2

D3

45° miter (typical)

A2

A1

8"

O

Q

N

J

I

L

Cut elongated biscuit slots at sides

1-1/4" fhws

H   K

G

F   G

3" overhang (right side)

3/4" deep dovetail mortise

B3

B2

B1

C

3"

E2   5"

1"

E1   E2

3" connector bolt and cap nut

8"

3"   3"   12"   3"   3"

1 x 1" bevel

1/4" chamfer (typical)

SECTION AT BOTTOM

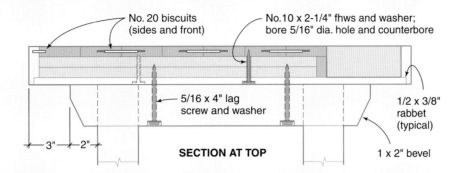

No. 20 biscuits (sides and front)

No.10 x 2-1/4" fhws and washer; bore 5/16" dia. hole and counterbore

5/16 x 4" lag screw and washer

1/2 x 3/8" rabbet (typical)

SECTION AT TOP

1 x 2" bevel

3" 2"

Shopping List

- ☐ 1×4 × 8-ft. pine boards (10)
- ☐ 1×6 × 8-ft. pine boards (2)
- ☐ 1×2 × 8-ft. pine board (1)
- ☐ 1×4 × 8-ft. maple boards (10)
- ☐ ³⁄₄-in. × 4×8 MDF (1)
- ☐ ½-in. × 5×5 Baltic birch plywood (1)
- ☐ 1¼-in. brads or staples
- ☐ No. 20 biscuits
- ☐ 3-in. connector bolts and caps
- ☐ 1⅝-in. flathead wood screws and finish washers
- ☐ ⁵⁄₁₆ × 4-in. lag screws and washers
- ☐ No. 10 × 2-in. screws and washers
- ☐ Wood glue
- ☐ Tung oil

Base Cutting List

Part/Description		No.	Size
A1	Outer leg, pine	8	¾ × 3 × 28½ in.
A2	Inner leg, pine	8	¾ × 3 × 34½ in.
B1	Outer foot, pine	4	¾ × 3 × 24 in.
B2	Center inner foot, pine	4	¾ × 3 × 12 in.
B3	End inner foot, pine	8	¾ × 3 × 3 in.
C	Foot pads, pine	4	¾ × 3 × 4 in.
D1	Outer top rail, pine	4	¾ × 3 × 22 in.
D2	Center inner top rail, pine	4	¾ × 3 × 12 in.
D3	End inner top rail, pine	8	¾ × 3 × 2 in.
E1	Outer stretcher, pine	2	¾ × 5 × 43 in.
E2	Inner stretcher, pine	2	¾ × 5 × 37 in.

Shelves Cutting List

Part	Description	No.	Size
F	Lower shelf, Baltic birch plywood	1	½ × 15⅛ × 37 in.
G	Lower shelf edging, pine	2	¾ × 1½ × 37 in.
H	Upper shelf bottom, Baltic birch plywood	1	½ × 5 × 36 in.
I	Upper shelf sides, Baltic birch plywood	2	½ × 4 × 5 in.
J	Upper shelf front, Baltic birch plywood	1	½ × 2 × 37 in.
K	Upper shelf back, Baltic birch plywood	1	½ × 4 × 37 in.

Top Cutting List

Part	Description	No.	Size
L	Top, maple	7	¾ × 3 × 59 in.*
M	Top frame front and back, maple	1	¾ × 2¾ × 60 in.**
N	Top frame sides, maple	2	¾ × 2¾ × 28 in.**
O	Substrate, MDF	2	¾ × 20¼ × 58½ in.
P	Top inside frame, maple	3	¾ × 1½ × 58½ in.
Q	Top/bottom, Baltic birch plywood	1	½ × 27¼ × 59¼ in.
R	Tool tray ramps, maple	5	¾ × 5½ × 4⅜ in.
S	Ramp cleats, Baltic birch plywood	6	½ × 1⅜ × 2¼ in.

* Finished panel is 21 × 58½ in.
** Length is from longest point to longest point.

By stripping away unnecessary design details, I created a woodworker's bench that performs all of the functions of a traditional bench, but mine is made of less expensive materials and takes less time to build. Standard ¾-in. lumber and simple joinery keep the cost down and make this an attractive project for woodworkers with limited tools. Stack-laminating the base-frame mortise-and-tenon joints makes the joinery process quick and easy without sacrificing strength. Woodworkers of all skill levels can confidently build this rock-solid bench.

THE DESIGN

You can build this bench out of almost any wood. It's best to use a hardwood such as maple for the top, but the base can be made from any solid stock — I chose pine. To minimize wood movement and achieve a consistent appearance, select boards with a straight grain pattern and similar color. I bought all of the materials (see Shopping List, p. 155) at a local home center.

The bench's footprint is 28 × 60 in., making it small enough to fit in almost any shop but large enough for most woodworking tasks. You can place it against a wall or in the center of the room, and it's easy to disassemble for moving or storage. I made

mine 38 in. tall because that is a comfortable working height for me, but you can adjust the leg lengths to suit your needs. You might consider making the height the same as or slightly lower than your table saw so the bench can act as an outfeed or side table.

This wouldn't be a woodworker's bench without vises. We chose a Veritas Twin Screw end vise and a Jorgensen woodworker's vise. Add bench-dog holes to further expand your vise's capacity and to hold work steady on the top.

Additional features include a tool tray to keep small tools and hardware within reach but off of the work surface. A shelf between the legs provides a place to put glue bottles, boxes of screws and nails, and a removable lower shelf is designed to hold toolboxes and cases.

THE BASE AND SHELVES

I achieved the look and strength of thick base stock by face gluing 1× stock to make the 1½- and 3-in.-thick legs, feet, top rail and stretchers.

Start the assembly with the legs. Center the two outer leg pieces over both sides of the two inner leg pieces to form the 3-in. tenons at each end of the leg. Glue and clamp the parts together. After the glue has cured, remove the excess glue with a scraper or chisel.

The stretchers and legs are assembled with a dovetail halving joint (see drawing detail, p. 154). I used a band saw to cut the dovetailed ends of the outer stretcher parts, but a jigsaw or handsaw will also work. Glue the stretcher parts together **(Photo A)**.

After the glue has cured, hold the stretchers against the legs as a template for you to mark the dovetail pro-

Glue the stretcher parts together, lining up the ends of the inner stretcher with the dovetail shoulders that you cut on the outer stretcher. Spread a thin layer of glue on one face, and use a damp cloth to wet the mating face.

Cut dovetail mortises in the legs. Clamp straightedges to the leg, and remove ¾ in. of material in three passes.

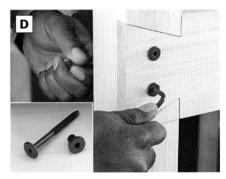

Carefully line up the laminations when gluing the feet and top rails to the legs. Glue and staple one piece in place at a time, and then clamp the entire assembly.

Fasten the leg assemblies and stretchers together with connector bolts (see inset). Use glue to reinforce this joint if you don't plan to disassemble the bench.

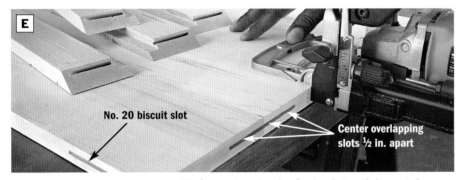

No. 20 biscuit slot

Center overlapping slots ½ in. apart

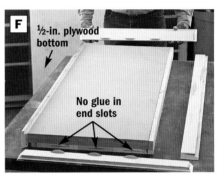

½-in. plywood bottom

No glue in end slots

Cut three No. 20 biscuit slots in the side frames (see drawing for details), and then cut three overlapping biscuit slots to form elongated slots in the maple top side edges.

Glue the front and inner frame pieces to the top assembly. Apply glue only to the miters of the side frame pieces.

file on the leg. Use a router to remove the material between the layout marks to a depth of ¾ in. **(Photo B)**.

Now assemble the foot parts around the bottom leg tenons **(Photo C)**. Do the same with the top rail parts and the upper leg tenons. Measure the leg assembly diagonally from corner to corner to ensure it is square. Then use the router to cut a ¼-in. chamfer on four edges of each foot pad, and attach the pads to the bottoms of the feet.

Finish the base assembly by fastening the legs to the stretchers with 3-in. connector bolts **(Photo D)**. Do not apply glue to this connection if you plan to disassemble the workbench in the future.

I used Baltic birch plywood for both shelves. One 5 × 5-ft. piece (a typical size for this type of plywood) is all you need. If it's not available in your area, you can substitute ½-in. AC-grade plywood. Fasten the upper shelf between the legs with screws, and rest the lower shelf on the stretchers.

THE TOP

A stable, flat work surface is essential for any bench. Traditional woodworking benches feature thick, solid tops, often made from 2- to 3-in.-thick quartersawn maple. I used ¾-in.-thick maple for the

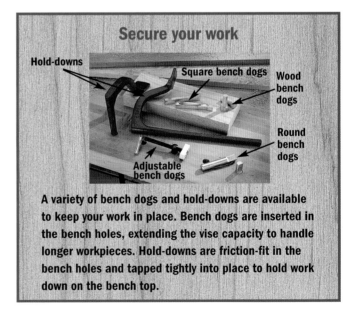

Secure your work

Hold-downs

Square bench dogs

Wood bench dogs

Round bench dogs

Adjustable bench dogs

A variety of bench dogs and hold-downs are available to keep your work in place. Bench dogs are inserted in the bench holes, extending the vise capacity to handle longer workpieces. Hold-downs are friction-fit in the bench holes and tapped tightly into place to hold work down on the bench top.

top surface and two layers of ¾-in. MDF as a substrate. The maple provides a hard work surface that can be sanded or planed when it becomes worn, and the MDF provides a stable and hefty backing. The bottom of the top is a ½-in. piece of birch plywood that also acts as the tray bottom.

The top assembly is designed to keep the maple

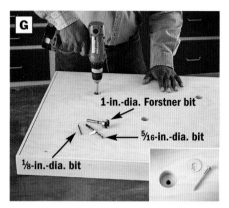

Three bits are used to create the countersink and pilot holes in the top assembly. First, bore the countersink with a 1-in.-dia. Forstner bit. Next, bore the oversize pilot hole with a ⁵⁄₁₆-in.-dia. bit. Finally, bore a ½-in.-deep pilot hole in the maple top with a ⅛-in.-dia. bit.

Use a scrap board as a carrier to safely cut the steep 30-degree ramp angles on a table saw. Cut the 60-degree bevel on the other end using a compound miter saw.

Fasten the vises to the underside of the bench with lag screws. Use shims to position the top of the vises flush with the top of the bench.

top flat and still allow wood movement. The top is glued only to the MDF along the front edge of the bench, which keeps the front edge flush. Biscuits are glued in the top and are not glued in the elongated slots in the side frames. And, the center and back edge of the top are held in place by screws driven through oversize screw holes in the MDF.

Carefully select surfaced maple that is straight and has smooth edges. Cut No. 20 biscuit slots on the edges of the top panel pieces; then glue up the panel. When the glue has cured, plane, scrape or sand the top flat and trim the ends to final size.

Before cutting the frame pieces to their final lengths, use a table saw or router to cut ½-in.-wide × ⅜-in.-deep rabbets along the bottom edge of each frame piece. Then miter the pieces to final length and cut slots for No. 0 biscuits in each miter.

Next, line up and cut No. 20 biscuit slots in the front and side top frame and front edge of the top. Then cut elongated slots in the side edges of the maple top **(Photo E)**.

I found it easiest to assemble the top upside down. Spread glue on the first few inches along the front edge of the maple top. Then place one of the MDF pieces on the top, keeping it flush against the front. Now spread glue over the exposed MDF surface, wet the face of the second sheet of MDF and place the second MDF piece on top. Clamp the three pieces, using cauls to distribute pressure over the entire surface.

While the panel assembly is curing, glue biscuits into the side frames. Gluing these biscuits in advance will prevent them from accidentally adhering to the maple top during the final assembly.

Finally, attach the frame parts to the top assembly **(Photo F)** and then spread a layer of glue over the

bottom MDF surface and in the rabbets, and position the ½-in. plywood bottom. Clamp the top assembly together. When the glue has cured, remove the clamps and drill six countersink and pilot holes through the top assembly. Stop the pilot holes before you bore into the maple top. Secure the top with No. 10 × 2-in. screws and washers centered in the oversize holes **(Photo G)**.

Small ramps in each end of the tool tray make cleaning it easier. Bevel-cut the 30- and 60-degree ends in each tool tray ramp **(Photo H)**. Attach the cleats and ramps; then you're ready to mount the top to the base.

Attach the top with two countersunk ⁵⁄₁₆- × 4-in. lag bolts and washers through each top rail/leg assembly. If you intend to leave the bench permanently assembled, apply glue between the top and base.

FINISHING TOUCHES

Apply a few coats of tung oil to the bench and it's ready to use as is, but adding a couple of vises greatly increases its utility **(Photo I)**.

Mounting the vises can be a project in itself. For example, the hefty Twin Screw end vise we chose required very precise hardware positioning. For specific instructions, refer to the vise's installation manual.

The final step is to drill ¾-in.-dia. bench-dog holes in line with the each vise. Space the holes apart half the distance of the vise's total capacity. Now you're ready to put the bench to work on your next project.

Vern Grassel, *writer*
Mark Macemon, *photography*
Patrick Gibson, *production assistance*
Gabriel Graphics, *illustration*

Index

31901046185890